YOU CAN'T LEAD

WITH YOUR FEET ON THE DESK

BUILDING RELATIONSHIPS, BREAKING DOWN BARRIERS, AND DELIVERING PROFITS

EDWIN D. FULLER

WILEY

John Wiley & Sons, Inc.

Published by John Wiley & Sons, Inc., Hoboken, New Jersey.
Published simultaneously in Canada.

For general information on our other products and services or for technical support, please contact our Customer Care Department within the United States at (800) 762-2974, outside the United States at (317) 572-3993 or fax (317) 572-4002.

Wiley also publishes its books in a variety of electronic formats. Some content that appears in print may not be available in electronic books. For more information about Wiley products, visit our web site at www.wiley.com.

Library of Congress Cataloging-in-Publication Data:

Fuller, Edwin D., 1945-
  You can't lead with your feet on the desk: building relationships, breaking down barriers, and delivering profits/Edwin D. Fuller.
     p. cm.
  ISBN 978-0-470-87961-0 (cloth)
  ISBN 978-1-118-00309-1 (ebk)
  ISBN 978-1-118-00310-7 (ebk)
  ISBN 978-1-118-00311-4 (ebk)
  1. Customer relations. 2. Business communication. 3. Leadership. 4. Success in business.
  I. Title. II. Title: You can't lead with your feet on the desk.
  HF5415.5.F865 2011
  658.4'092—dc22

                                                                            2010036015

Printed in the United States of America

10 9 8 7 6 5 4 3 2

To the International Pioneers, the 72,000 associates of Marriott's International Lodging Division, my mentors, peers, Thaddeus, and Heidi Ann.

Marsha, Anna, and Josh, thank you for completing me.

Contents

Foreword

Too many businesses today are out of balance. They are focused on short-term results achieved through impersonal transactional negotiations where deals are concluded solely on price with little or no personal interaction and no relationship-building. This is a big mistake. At the end of the day, it's the people in the organization and the *way* they do business that makes the difference.

"People First" has always been the bedrock of Marriott International, from the day in 1927 when my parents opened their nine-seat root beer stand in Washington, DC, to today as an enterprise of more than 3,500 hotels in 70 countries across the globe. By listening to, respecting, valuing, and celebrating people over our 83 years, we have created inclusive environments in which the talents and ideas of millions of our guests, employees, partners, property owners, and various other stakeholders worldwide have contributed to our "Spirit to Serve" culture and helped us earn an unassailable competitive advantage.

Whether you're the leader of a mega-enterprise, the owner of the local corner drugstore, or a young executive just starting out, your ultimate success will, more often than not, depend on the mutual respect and care you consistently demonstrate for the people around you. Usually, it's the salespeople who take the time to know their customers and understand their needs who win the business. Similarly, it's the manager who consistently turns in good numbers and radiates energy and enthusiasm who often gets the nod for a promotion. But even more impressive is the manager who also knows his or her entire staff by name (without checking the nametag) and is spontaneously greeted with smiles, teasing, and hellos. For me, the relationship our general managers have with their teams is the litmus test of how well a hotel is run.

That kind of "relationships first" spirit is what has helped Ed Fuller, the head of Marriott International Lodging, grow the business from 16 hotels to 400, in 70 countries. It's also the major theme in this insightful and entertaining book. Ed shares scores of personal anecdotes from a 40-year corporate career, along with those of other leaders, that illustrate how deep personal relationships built on mutual respect and trust, and nurtured over time, can save a volatile business deal, inspire team members to greatness, ensure service excellence, bridge cultural divides, and create a long-term, profitable business.

Ed suggests how listening carefully to discern the other person's hidden motivations can help you find solutions to a seemingly insurmountable impasse, how you can set the ground rules for a productive business relationship even when you have nothing in common with the other person, and why having a solid core value system can support your efforts and outline the ethical boundaries within virtually any relationship.

As Ed emphasizes, relationships are the currency of every culture and they are rarely formed while sitting behind the desk. I still make it a point to spend much of my time on the road, visiting our hotels, meeting with industry leaders and calling on customers. This allows me to counter the notion that big corporations are faceless machines. I also want to show our team in the field that I value their work enough to take time to check it out. At the same time, visiting with our customers year in and year out provides me with a strong knowledge base for making decisions.

So, get out from behind your desk, your phone, or your shop counter. You'll be amazed with what you learn, with the positive impact you can make, and by the opportunities that most assuredly will come your way.

—J.W. Marriott, Chairman and CEO
of Marriott International

Acknowledgments

In creating this book for you there have been a number of contributors some I have mentioned in the text of the book. I'd like to thank my mentors and peers who helped me develop my philosophy and concepts for this book. I especially want to acknowledge Marriott International's Global Pioneers whose untiring dedication enabled me to lead the growth of our business over the past 21 years.

THE GLOBAL PIONEERS

Linda Bartlett, Harry Bosschaart, Stan Bruns, Nuala Cashman, Paul Cerula, Weili Cheng, Don Cleary, Mark Conklin, JoAnn Cordary, Henry Davies, Victoria Dolan, Brenda Durham, Ron Eastman, Joel Eisemann, June Farrell, Franz Ferschke, Jim Fisher, Fern Fitzgerald, Paul Foskey, Geoff Garside, Robert Gaymer-Jones, Jürgen Giesbert, Marc Gulliver, Tracy Halphide, Pat Henderson, Jeff Holdaway, Andrew Houghton, Ed Hubennette, Gary Hurst, Beth Irons, Andrea Jones, Pam Jones, Simon Jongert, Nihad Kattan, Kevin Kearney, Chuck Kelley, Karl Kilburg, Tuni Kyi, Henry Lee, Mike Mackie, Alastair McPhail, Scott Melby, Raj Menon, Anton Najjar, JP Nel, Scott Neumayer, John Northen, Jim O'Hern, Alan Orlob, Manuel Ovies, Jim Pilarski, Belinda Pote, Barbara Powell, Gary Rosenthal,

Reiner Sachau, Mark Satterfield, Brenda Shelton, Craig Smith, Brad Snyder, Alex Stadlin, Peter Steger, Tim Sylvester, Susan Thronson, Myron Walker, Hank Weigle, and Glenn Wilson.

Several people encouraged me to write down my ideas and experiences: Roger Dow, June Farrell, Debbie Harrison, Pam Jones, Kevin Kimball, Kathleen Matthews, Andy Policano, Marsha Scarbrough, Bill Shaw, Arne Sorenson, Jim Stamas, Pat Stocker, Carl Wilson, Glenn Wilson, and Steve Weisz. Their support and advice played a critical role in convincing me to sit down and write the words.

I can't thank enough those who kept me going and guided me once I got started: Katie Bianchi, Yvonne Bean, Donna Carpenter, Mo Coyle, Buck Laird, Helen Rees, and Bob Watts.

And finally, there are simply no words to describe my enduring thanks to Brenda Shelton, my right arm (and sometimes my left), who has taken this journey with me for the past 35 years.

I hope their encouragement and hard work will benefit you the reader.

Chapter 1 Ditch the Desk

A desk is a dangerous place from which to view the world.

— John le Carré

No one would ever confuse me with George Clooney, but I have accomplished something that Ryan Bingham, the character Clooney played in the movie, *Up in the Air*, coveted. By accumulating more than 10 million frequent-flyer miles, I earned the right to have my name painted on the fuselage of a United Airlines 747.

I was logging around 700,000 miles annually during the 1990s when we were launching Marriott's international lodging operations, and a good deal of my travel time was spent in the friendly skies of United. One year the airline came up with a unique promotion to reward 50 of its most frequent fliers. And that's how the words, "Ed Fuller, Customer," came to be painted beneath the pilot's window on a United 747.

As president and managing director of the Marriott division that operates and franchises overseas hotels, I spend a significant part of my life flying in and out of the scores of foreign countries where we conduct business. And my 10-million-plus miles have taught me a lot about the value of getting out from behind my desk and building relationships that span cultural differences.

I'm not unique. For any manager, knowledge of other cultures makes it easier to navigate the complexities of today's multicultural workplace. Whether you are managing a clothing factory, a customer call center, or a stock-and-bond trading operation, it's the rare business that doesn't depend on a diverse group of employees, overseas suppliers, and partners. With all these stakeholders, some understanding of other cultures is an important plank in the building of strong and productive relationships.

A case in point: For nearly 20 years, "Mohammed" had been a friend and business partner. We had shared journeys, meals, and considerable profits while weathering dozens of the disagreements that accompany any successful relationship, business or personal. Then came the day in 2009 when he glared at me and hissed, "Your company will be dead to me when you retire."

Our association had begun when Mohammed, a successful entrepreneur in the Middle East, decided to build a hotel and needed the management expertise we at Marriott International could provide. Given our long and fruitful history, his outburst was a shock but not a total surprise. Even the closest of business connections can be extraordinarily fragile when the interests of the two parties collide.

For many business leaders, the word *relationship* evokes excessive emotionalism, and smacks of the dread *soft stuff*. But not to my ears. During two decades of establishing and directing the international operations of the Marriott hotel chain—a period in which we went from 16 hotels in six countries grossing $325 million to our current 400 properties scattered across 70 countries and with revenues of nearly $7 billion—I've witnessed the rise and fall of many an enterprise and many a leader. Experience has taught me that, far from being irrelevant, solid relationships are the real bedrock of business success. They can help you solve problems and resolve contentious issues amicably. Relationships are especially important in emerging economies, where a handshake often serves as a valid contract and where written documents are a necessary, if unwelcome, part of doing business with Americans and other Westerners.

Solid relationships are not formed overnight; however, and they are defined by culture and community. Different values and customs can sometimes make genuine connections difficult to build and maintain. In any event, it will take time and effort to cement a bond. And that doesn't happen behind a desk.

A strong connection may begin with untold hours of dining together and mingling at social events. But to reinforce a productive relationship, you need to demonstrate fairness and evenhandedness—which is more difficult than you might think in those cultures where win-lose solutions are deemed preferable to win-wins. And even then, the risk of missteps and misperceptions is never far away. It's hard work to be sure, but the rewards of getting out from behind your desk and building strong relationships face-to-face are many.

As my crisis with Mohammed demonstrated, however, even after years spent developing trust and confidence, a relationship can be damaged in one disagreeable moment. Our falling-out had its start in a financial dispute between Mohammed and his partners and our neutral stance on the matter.

In subsequent visits, I took pains to assure Mohammed of our respect and admiration and told him we had considered a variety of possible solutions. Nevertheless, he remained frustrated by his predicament, and he eventually told me that the real issue was our refusal to unquestioningly take his side in the quarrel. The depth of our relationship was the only thing that kept the partnership from breaking apart. It allowed us to get beyond the emotions and cultural differences that could have made the rupture permanent. Eventually, the dispute found resolution, but the need to ditch the desk and maintain the relationship remained.

The story of Mohammed resonates across the business landscape. In today's borderless world, the ability to create lasting connections is crucial to every business leader—and maintaining those cross-cultural relationships demands a pragmatic flexibility that isn't taught in business schools.

I wrote this book to share the lessons I've learned over 20 years—almost none of them spent behind a desk— developing and tending relationships in dozens of countries. I've also drawn on the experiences of other businesspeople and well-known figures whose leadership has produced tremendous results. Many of the personal insights and techniques I describe in these pages are the products of trial and error, with the emphasis on error. They have proven their value over many years, and I hope that you'll find them equally useful.

THE WORLD BEYOND THE DESK

Most business leaders need only drive to a plant in a neighboring county or ride the elevator to the ground-floor loading dock to see and appreciate cultural differences. In other words, if you are spending your days meeting with other managers or sitting at your desk doing paperwork, it's time to broaden your horizons and get closer to your business.

Building successful business relationships is no different than building personal ones. It demands meaningful engagement with another party. When I was assigned to build the Marriott International organization, my most challenging relationships were with some of the company's leaders: They had precious little time or resources for our fledgling unit, given that virtually all of Marriott's operations were based in the United States.

Worse still, our American focus meant that all of our policies and systems were geared to the requirements of our

U.S. hotels. That was a problem because what we needed abroad was often quite different from what we had at home. Standards had to be adjusted to meet local customer requirements. For example, we needed prayer rooms in Muslim countries, two equal-size ballrooms to separately accommodate men and women at weddings and other celebrations in the Middle East, more restaurants catering to local tastes and ingredients, varied types of food preparation, and flexible smoking policies, to name a few.

Initially, I did anything I could to get people at headquarters to think globally, including even offering to pay $20 to anyone who used the word *global*. I'd happily pull out $20 from my wallet when someone qualified, which wasn't often. Then I went to a meeting at which our CEO Bill Marriott Jr. used *global* six times in his presentation. When he finished, he turned to me and said: "All right, Ed, that will be $120."

We also initiated what I called Iron Bird Tours that took senior executives on 10-day jaunts around the world to visit our hotels and resorts and those of competitors. The trips gave our top people the opportunity to experience different cultures—and customers. Executives could also participate in a four-week education program, one week of which was devoted to global issues. A week-long course in Costa Rica, for example, included a two-hour visit with the country's president, Nobel Peace Prize winner Oscar Arias. I led the Iron Bird trips for several years (more about that in Chapter 3) and taught in most of our executive education programs. Over time, my colleagues—and the company as a whole—began to internalize a wider global perspective.

Marriott traces its beginnings to a nine-stool A&W root beer stand that John Willard Marriott and Alice Sheets

Marriott opened in Washington, DC, in 1927, just months after their marriage in Utah. Soon, they added Mexican food to the menu and renamed their business the Hot Shoppe, which they expanded into a chain.

Bill and Alice were well acquainted with hard work. As a youngster, Bill had helped his father raise sugar beets and sheep on the family's small farm, and Alice had helped her widowed mother keep house. Bill was just 13 when he was given the responsibility of planting, raising, and harvesting crops on a few acres entrusted to him by his father. A year later, on his own, he took 3,000 head of sheep to market in San Francisco.

He held his managers at the Hot Shoppes to his own high standards of performance. He was known for standing beside employees while they worked and quizzing them about company procedures. If a cook failed to come up with the right answer to how many times hash brown potatoes should be turned—once—the cook could expect to be grilled himself on every aspect of his work.

At its peak, the chain offered more than 300 items on its menu. Bill Sr. demanded that every item be fresh and available 24 hours a day, 7 days a week. That forced the managers to occasionally take extraordinary measures. If the boss showed up at one of the restaurants and ordered a dish that wasn't on hand, its manager would immediately call nearby Hot Shoppes to locate the missing comestible. Once it was found, arrangements would be made for runners from each restaurant to meet at some halfway point and pass the food baton.

One of the most fundamental competitive advantages enjoyed by Hot Shoppes—and by later Marriott enterprises as well—is their consistency. Every detail of every aspect of an operation is painstakingly studied and a "best" way of proceeding is developed and set down for all to follow. The resulting guides provide the ground rules that make it possible for employees to deliver consistently high levels of service. One entry lays out 66 steps to thoroughly clean a hotel room in less than 30 minutes. The result: Whether you're registered at a Marriott in Minneapolis or Monaco, you're going to get the same service—and you're going to want to register at a Marriott wherever you travel.

In 1937, Bill Sr. literally took a flyer on a new business. He had been making one of his unannounced visits to a Hot Shoppe near Hoover Airfield outside Washington, DC, when he saw that many the customers were buying sandwiches and coffee to take along on their flights. In short order, as it were, he sat down with Eddie Rickenbacker, the World War I ace who was the head of Eastern Air Transport, offering to deliver ready-to-eat boxed lunches to Eastern's passengers. Rickenbacker bit. In-Flite Catering delivered its first meals that same year to flights out of Hoover, a site currently occupied by the Pentagon. In-Flite would eventually become the largest airline catering business in the world.

Bill Sr. was constantly looking for new opportunities. Over time the company began providing food for hospitals and schools. It acquired the concessions to provide meals within airports. It bought restaurant chains—Roy Rogers and Bob's Big Boy among them—and resort properties.

In the 1970s, when sales at some of the older Hot Shoppes on toll roads began to fade, the company recognized the latent power of its newer brands. The floundering Shoppes were turned over to Big Boy or Roy Rogers, and business once again boomed. It wasn't long before the managers of Marriott's concession business adopted that same branding strategy, bringing national chains like Pizza Hut into its airport operations.

In the Marriott family's drive for perfection, there actually came a time when, having developed industry-leading processes to manage its various divisions, the company began to sell its expertise to outsiders. Its distribution system, for example, responsible for shipping food and supplies to widespread holdings, gave Marriott a major cost advantage over its competitors. That fact inspired the family to create Marriott Distribution Services, which became a $1 billion business delivering food from 13 distribution centers across the country to such clients as Boston Chicken and Steak and Ale.

The Marriotts first entered the hotel business in January 1958 with the opening of the Twin Bridges in Arlington, Virginia. As usual, the family was a hands-on presence. Bill Jr. described the scene this way: "Mother, Dad, and I stayed up half the night hanging pictures so we could check in guests the next day in time for President Eisenhower's second inauguration."

The decision to take on the Twin Bridges was a prescient and gutsy one. The family had no real experience with the industry, and the hotel, with its 365 rooms, was a tough place to start. "We were flying by the seat of our pants," is how Bill Jr. put it. One of his first tasks was to find ways to cut expenses. Under an item called "other," he found a substantial sum charged for ice buckets. The sturdy wax-covered cardboard buckets the hotel was using, which cost a dollar each, were being toted off by guests. He replaced them with permanent ice buckets for each room.

After he became president in 1964, Bill Jr. switched the company's focus from food service to lodging. Within six years, the company's hotel holdings soared nearly fourfold, lifting its revenues and profits above those of Howard Johnson and Hilton Hotels, the giants of the time.

Generally speaking, the company acquired or built its hotels and then managed them. Then, in the late 1970s, we adopted a model in which we built our hotels and sold the buildings to other companies, often insurance companies or other institutions, with the proviso that we would manage the properties for a fee. The strategy worked well until the recession of the early 1990s caught us with more than $2 billion in hotel assets under construction. We weathered the downturn with great difficulty.

At the same time, we started expanding into international lodging, laying down a basic strategy that has been followed ever since with few exceptions: Third parties build and own the hotels, and we provide the brand, services, and management, collecting a base fee and an incentive fee determined by the hotel's profits. We also expanded our franchise activities and embraced a multiple brand strategy. Today, Marriott is comprised of more than 18 brands, ranging from Courtyard to Fairfield Inn & Suites to the Ritz-Carlton.

We were forced to override our international no ownership rule early in the 1990s when we were trying to break into new markets in Asia, Europe, and Latin and South America. We entered into 20 joint ventures because it was impossible to get a hotel built in Hong Kong, Frankfurt, or Chile, to name a few places, without our direct financial investment or some sort of leasing vehicle. To reach our goal of expanding to six continents, we had to build a strategically focused, international business model practically from scratch. We did it by merging leadership, training, clean lines of responsibility, and an emphasis on accountability with our clear set of corporate principles, proving that the "Marriott Way" could deliver exceptional value overseas just as it had done back home.

We started by laying out our governing strategies, asking: Which of the Marriott brands should lead the way? Where did we want to establish our first hotels?

The brand question was easily answered given that, in the early 1990s, we had only one full-service brand, Marriott. We knew it would draw international travelers and create a positive impression for our other, smaller brands—the so-called *halo effect*.

I came to understand the power of strong brands when I was based in Chicago running Marriott's Midwest division in 1986. We operated a good, medium-quality property near the Bloomington, Minnesota, airport. Then we acquired the 602-room Amfac Hotel in nearby Minneapolis. The Amfac was the city's premier hotel. It housed three restaurants and was the preferred venue for society events. We were still in the process of rebranding when two of the town's prominent citizens stopped in to say they were planning to move their annual charity ball to another venue. With nothing but their impression of the airport hotel to guide them, they didn't think Marriott could handle an elegant event. We changed their perception by introducing them to our top-flight operations in other cities.

Our strategy overseas would begin with placing top-quality, highly visible hotels in key capital cities, thus showcasing our premier product and smoothing the way for lower-profile brands to enter secondary markets. It's what I call the "billboard" effect. Leading with your most prominent brands creates a positive impression. And in the hospitality business, positive impressions go wherever your guests go—from big-city markets to smaller ones and back again.

Deciding where to make our international debut was the next question. Our key source markets provided the answer. Source markets are those that typically produce the largest number of international travelers. In the early 1990s, the United States, Japan, Germany, the United Kingdom, and France were the top five source markets. The United States led not because most Americans had passports—fewer than 15 percent did then and only 25 percent do now—but because of the size of our population.

We wanted to do business in these countries because of the spectacular potential for growth and because of a little-known fact about the lodging business: When travelers book rooms abroad, they look for hotel brands they recognize or have patronized in their own countries. For example, first-time Japanese travelers to the United States usually book a room at a Hilton. Hilton entered the Japanese market years before any other lodging company, so Japanese travelers know the brand. If we wanted to corral a considerable number of global travelers at any of our properties, we would have to establish a noticeable presence in the key countries.

We did just that, making ourselves a visible part of the lodging landscape one target country at a time.

GETTING IT DONE

Through the years I have developed a set of guidelines for building relationships with my team members, hotel owners, associates, and guests. The guidelines are somewhat fluid, depending on the nature of the connection and the people involved. There is just one ironclad rule: You must consider the other person's interests and needs.

As I travel the world, I often find myself sitting beside a hotel manager or owner at an elaborate dinner attended by dozens of the community's most prominent citizens. Sometimes my role is simply to be there so the owner can show off to local businesspeople and the political elite. It's not me he's interested in as much as my title. "See, I have the president of Marriott Lodging International with me," he or she is saying. The owner's association with Marriott bestows prominence and power in the community and opens up fresh opportunities for him or her.

"Don't you feel like a figurehead?" my U.S. friends occasionally ask. No. My goal is to create and cement a relationship, and if my presence can further that goal, I am going to show up.

I am reminded of my friend Sam Huff, a gentleman, though the bruisers who encountered him on the football field in the 1950s and 1960s would surely dispute the term *gentle*. Sam was a New York Giants' star who pioneered the middle linebacker position and showed how defense could win games. All-NFL three times, chosen for five Pro Bowls, and an early inductee into the Pro Football Hall of Fame, Sam's exploits were featured in a *Time* magazine cover story and a Walter Cronkite special called, "The Violent World of Sam Huff."

Sam finished his gridiron career with the Washington Redskins, at which point Bill Marriott hired him as a salesman, initially to attract on-the-road sports teams to our hotels. When I became a Marriott salesman, calling on potential customers, Sam worked with me on my most important insurance accounts. Many of our younger salespeople didn't want his help. They saw Sam as a competitor, did not understand his value, and insisted they didn't need him. If a sale were made, they had no desire to share the credit.

I thought they were wrong. The executives we called on were usually from an earlier generation. My father, for example, considered Sam a hero. When I finagled a sales call to the president of New York Life, for instance, I knew that without Sam, I would have been left to cool my heels in the outer office. With Sam along, the receptionist ushered us right into the president's office.

Sam shared a few football stories—how he stopped Jim Brown on the one-yard line or intercepted a pass to seal a Giants' victory. At a certain point—always perfectly timed—he gave the president a little sales pitch for the hotel, saying, "You know, Ed here needs some leads to book meetings at Marriott hotels." The president buzzed his assistant to send in the company's meeting planner, and we walked out with a full calendar of events. Sam's pitch worked almost every time.

One night, Sam and I got to talking at a (Marriott hotel, of course) bar. He said I was lucky because I would reach the peak of my career when I was older and wiser, whereas he had hit the top early and would most likely never fly so high again. That didn't mean, he rushed to add, that he wasn't still working at it.

True, Sam was no longer in the spotlight, but he was proud of his work and understood the importance that relationships played in business success. He also understood better than most how to get out from behind his desk, connect with people, and turn that connection into sales and profits. Thanks to this wise man, I booked dozens of meetings, and Sam was at the top of his game in my eyes.

I've spent considerable time with another enormously famous person who has demonstrated the value of relationships in a very different universe. My life intersects with that of Charles, the Prince of Wales, on two fronts—environmental sustainability and creating opportunities for young people. His International Tourism Partnership (ITP) focuses the major lodging chains on those objectives.

At Marriott we're committed to preserving the environment and supporting nonprofit green organizations around the world. One of our initiatives is aimed at halting the destruction of Brazil's rain forests. Working with local governments, our contribution, bolstered by gifts solicited from our guests and employees, help us pay people in remote villages to protect trees rather than cut them down. As Bill Marriott put it, "We realize that we are all guests on this planet, [and] we're very concerned about climate change."

I have been privileged to represent the company at various environmental events hosted by Prince Charles and have served as ITP chairman for 8 of my 16 years on its board. Our first encounter was at Highgrove House, the country estate Charles transformed into an organic farm and garden. I was among a dozen people, primarily corporate types, who followed him on a tour of his garden, which includes a meadow planted with more than 30 varieties of endangered native plants, everything from yellow rattle to meadow crane's bill.

After the tour, we wound up in the kitchen around a long table. I sat across from Charles as he spoke passionately about the importance of preserving our planet's natural heritage. His devotion to the topic frequently draws disdain in the press, but when you see him in person, you realize he's just a fellow—a special fellow, to be sure—trying to do the right thing.

Prince Charles is, in my estimation, a convener with a twist: He brings people together as all relationship-builders do, but because of his position and personality, he can facilitate connections between disparate individuals that serve a larger purpose. People who might otherwise have little or no interest in environmental issues end up working to make their organizations greener because of his intervention.

At the same time, the relationships that emerge can further the participants' particular priorities. At one of my sessions with Prince Charles, I was able to discuss Marriott business with Charles Petruccelli, the president of Global Travel Services for American Express. Our discussion led to the untangling of a perplexing problem affecting both companies.

In short, relationships are the currency of every culture. Whether the connections are made and cultivated by a prince working to help his favorite charities or by a CEO hoping to win the loyalty of his associates, the bonds between people are a company's lifeblood, the wax used to seal the social contract. And they rarely form behind a desk.

A story about Walt Disney shows what can go wrong when you don't understand the importance of relationships. Disney was clearly a genius. His movies, theme parks, and merchandising strategies changed the nature of entertainment around the world. But he was a genius with a tin ear when it came to relationships and cultural differences, and that shortcoming hurt his business at a crucial point.

Disney was a hot-tempered, tyrannical micromanager, a perfectionist whose attitude toward his people veered erratically from contempt to camaraderie. He appropriated and altered his artists' works, gave them no public credit, and set salaries and bonuses at his whim. Veteran animators were sometimes ordered to train novices, only to find that the newcomers were being paid more than they were. Not surprisingly, his studio in the late 1930s was a hotbed of discontent. Yet Disney saw himself as a benevolent leader. He was shocked when two-thirds of his animators went on strike. He felt betrayed and blamed communist agitators. In retaliation, Disney laid off more than 250 people and shut down the studio for a month rather than recognize the union. In the end, Disney lost the fight.

His reputation was saved by the studio's patriotic work in World War II, and he later cultivated the image of kindly Uncle Walt. But he never learned to bridge gaps or forge relationships, remaining an isolated figure who made all the decisions for his company—often against overwhelming opposition. His genius led him to win more often than he lost, but unless you're a certified prodigy, I wouldn't advise following his example.

THE ROAD AHEAD

Here's a preview of what's to come in the pages ahead.

- Chapter 2: "The Value of Values." No business relationship can survive and prosper unless at least one of the partners lives by a set of clear moral standards. I've seen firsthand how the value system laid down by Marriott's founder and maintained by his son has provided a firm structure on which to build relationships with stakeholders.
- Chapter 3: "To Respect Is to Inspire." Successful leadership requires mutual respect. If you want your associates or your partners to respect you, then you must learn to respect them—and their cultures, as well. One measure of respect for frontline people is a strong policy that dictates promotion from within.
- Chapter 4: "Trust Must Be Earned." The effectiveness of any leader, in business or otherwise, is a function of the level of trust he or she inspires. It takes time to win another person's trust, though you can speed up the process by coming through in an emergency. Crises offer a unique opportunity to cement a trusting relationship. When disaster, natural or man-made, hits one of our hotels anywhere in the world, I ditch the desk and get there fast.
- Chapter 5: "Learn to Communicate." The ability to clearly convey ideas and attitudes is crucial to being an effective leader. You need to monitor and hone your ability to communicate verbally and nonverbally. Did you know

that the clothes you wear to a meeting, along with the way you physically react to criticism, can make or break a relationship?

- Chapter 6: "Lead from the Front." To maintain the respect and trust of their teams, leaders must be willing and able to take on any assignment they might hand out to others. Occasionally, you must lead from the front by giving yourself tough jobs instead of handing them off to subordinates. In my case, leading from the front required me to take on the unenviable task of firing a longtime associate. I also accompanied my team to war-torn Iraq to check out potential hotel sites.

- Chapter 7: "The Past Lives On." The attitudes and behaviors of employees and customers raised abroad are, to a large degree, determined by their culture of origin. To create a positive relationship with them you need to develop some familiarity with their cultures. Often, what you might perceive as their inappropriate behavior is a product of prejudices rooted in history. An example from my bad playbook: Don't hire a Japanese manager to run a hotel in Korea.

- Chapter 8: "Cultivate Your Connections." In an ever-more-connected business world, relationships have become the new testing ground for leaders. Your skill at forming and retaining close ties with associates and partners is a competitive advantage. To make the most of that skill, organize your time to leave room for stay-in-touch phone calls to partners, impromptu sessions with your team, and occasional trips to outlying branch offices. Such actions will pay enormous dividends.

This book is mainly addressed to business leaders and others aspiring to become leaders and managers, because I believe they (or should I say you?) can benefit from my experience. But my central message regarding the value of relationship building across cultures, and the fieldwork and shoe leather it takes, has a far broader application.

The United States's attitude toward the rest of the world has undergone extreme swings over the centuries. Our physical segregation fostered an isolationist view that lasted, with occasional lapses, until World War II. But even as the United States built an empire in the Pacific and the Caribbean, we managed to maintain our feeling of separateness.

Our commitment to the defeat of the Axis powers and the postwar resurrection of Europe pretty much quieted any significant isolationist murmurings emanating from the U.S. political wings. It did not, however, erase our sense of independence and special identity—even though the information revolution of the past decade or two has made the world flat.

But the fact is, we can no longer afford to see ourselves as separate and independent. Increasingly, the world is coming to us, and we must deal with employees, suppliers, partners, and customers whose roots lie in other cultures. We cannot escape the fact that, like the rest of the world, we are linked economically to other countries. Huge potentially bankrupting quantities of our currency are in the hands of other nations. Some of them, namely China and India, are threatening our claim to scientific and technological leadership. Our political leadership is also under attack.

Given the shape of the world, it is long past time for U.S. business leaders, politicians, and citizens at large to reach beyond our immediate world to create strong, new relationships with our counterparts in other countries. These connections can achieve what the United Nations and other global organizations have not—a positive change in the basic attitudes and behavior of people toward each other.

My long experience working outside the United States has convinced me that the best way to gain a better, more complete understanding of people, cultures, beliefs, and historical events is to leave my desk behind. Too few of us venture outside our borders. When only a quarter of U.S. citizens owns a passport—which many use to visit Canada and Mexico, neighbors we already know—it's not hard to understand why most of us lack a broad, global perspective.

If we can build bridges, one relationship at a time, I believe we can take a giant step toward resolving some of the conflicts that are ravaging the world. Am I putting too much faith in the power of relationships? Some would say yes. But firsthand experience has shown me otherwise. Let's ditch the desk and get started.

Chapter 2 The Value of Values

The quality of a leader is reflected in the standards they set for themselves.

—Ray Kroc

We had reached an agreement with one of China's wealthiest real-estate investors. He would build a spectacular, full-service hotel in a major Chinese city, and we would operate it for him. Our people monitored his progress as the property began taking shape. They were not happy.

The owner's contractors were cutting corners. The building materials were second-rate, and the workmanship was slipshod. In a series of sessions involving various levels of our executive team, we delivered the same message: Marriott has high standards, and this particular property was not up to par.

We enlisted Henry Lee, our area vice president, to serve as point man. Henry's superb relationship skills were on display in a time-consuming series of lunches, meetings, and one-on-one conversations. Despite our importuning, though, the owner refused to change his approach.

Through it all, we never wavered. "Build the hotel the right way or we won't accept it," our team told the owner. He courteously responded, "Yes, you will."

A competing hotel had recently opened a substandard property, and our prospective owner thought we would follow suit. We refused. He held out for two years, terminating our contract eight times and rehiring us every time. He somehow managed to withstand the financial pressure to move ahead. Finally, the stalemate was broken when he realized that his contractors were letting him down and costing him a good deal of money by not doing the job right the first time.

"I hate what you people did," he told us, "but I respect you for doing it." We eventually opened his hotel, and it has been successful. The owner and our team understand each other better now.

Vigilantly upholding our standards is part of the value system the Marriott family established early in its 83-year history and has maintained ever since. When the dust settled with the Chinese owner, other owners of Marriott properties in the city told us they approved of our consistent stand. What they did not say—though it was clearly understood on all sides—was that if we had yielded to him, they would have looked foolish for agreeing to maintain our standards in the hotels they had previously built.

I believe that leaders in every field must stick to their values as both a moral imperative and a practical necessity. Long-lasting, productive business relationships are only possible if your behavior is responsible and consistently so. In a world where everyone is maneuvering to gain an advantage, inconsistency is intolerable.

TAKING RESPONSIBILITY

My early years gave little hint that I would end up leading a large organization. I was born in 1945 in Petersburg, Virginia, when my father, an Army captain, was stationed at nearby Fort Lee. After a stint in Gainesville, Florida, where my father sold high school and college class rings for the L.G. Balfour Company, we moved to Attleboro, Massachusetts, which was the headquarters of the Balfour Company.

I was a so-so student in high school, where I worked summers as a janitor. At Wake Forest University, my grades suffered because of the family battles that swirled around me, as an only child, when my parents divorced. The dean of students, Edwin Wilson, suggested that I withdraw in my sophomore year to preserve what grades I had.

I moved to Boston where I found work as a file clerk at the Lahey Clinic and attended Boston University's night school. Six months later, I became a full-time student there, aided by a letter to the school from Dean Wilson, but I was not happy. I felt lost and lonely among the school's 30,000 students. I was actually thinking of quitting when I was taken under the wing of two fellow students, Dave Trexler and Bob Watts. "Stick with us," they told me, "and you'll have plenty of friends and lots to do."

With their help, I joined the SAE fraternity and gradually learned how to build lasting relationships. I became business manager of a school newspaper and treasurer of the SAE fraternity. I took part in student government and was put in charge of Intra-fraternity Council rush, the recruiting function for all fraternities at Boston University, and ultimately I was elected a member of the Scarlet Key in recognition of my extracurricular work around the university. My grades improved as I became more active. It was my first taste of leadership, and I liked it. While at BU, I worked at the Prudential Center as a Pinkerton security guard. During special events I recruited my fraternity brothers to serve as special officers directing traffic. One week I served as part of Steve McQueen's personal body guard team while he was in town filming *The Thomas Crown Affair*.

Also while at BU, I continued in ROTC, which I had started at Wake Forest University. It kept me from being drafted into the Army, but on graduation in 1968 I entered active duty as a second lieutenant. When my initial training was complete, assignments were handed out. By design no one in the training unit got what he asked for, which laid the groundwork for the detailing officer who offered a deal of sorts, though with no guarantees: Sign up for an extra year, and you might get a posting you'll like. As a child, I had dreamed of becoming a pilot, but my eyesight wasn't good enough. My goal was to get into the aviation industry, so I signed on for the extra year of duty in hopes of getting a job running an aerial port operation, which involves moving military personnel in and out of a particular country. There was an opening in Frankfurt, Germany, and that's where I spent the next two years. With that posting, I was, for the first time, introduced to the cultures, customs, scents, flavors, and amazing sights to be found outside the United States.

My job responsibilities were equally eye-opening. I was a second lieutenant doing the work of a full colonel. I presided over an aerial port operation that oversaw the transport of 500,000 Army, Navy, and Coast Guard passengers and their families annually. The soldiers and sailors were on their way to Vietnam or back, heading for any of a hundred destinations. As a young lieutenant, I learned that I could bring change to one of the world's largest organizations—the U.S. Army.

Time and again I had to decide whether I would set standards for my team or let them take the easy route. In one case I discovered that two enlisted men and two officers from the Pennsylvania Army National Guard were flying all over Europe using invalid travel orders. In effect, they were taking seats from more deserving military personnel. Then I found out how they managed to do it: One of the four, a full colonel, was related to the Air Force commanding general of the military airlift command unit stationed on the airbase. If I blew the whistle, I was putting any future military career on the line, but I believed then—and believe to this day—that leaders have no choice in such situations.

I reported the case to the Army's criminal investigation division, which eventually indicted the four. Days later the

Air Force general gave me a 15-minute cussing out in the base parking lot. There would be no long-term career consequences, though, because my Army commander backed me for doing the right thing.

Most of my time in Vietnam was spent working with the South Vietnamese and Thai military and the Korean White Horse division units in the central highlands. It was dangerous duty. We were ambushed a number of times, took mortar fire many nights, and sometimes found ourselves in foxholes or behind a Jeep exchanging fire with the Vietcong. My decisions as a captain in the MAC-V (Military Assistance Command-Vietnam) sometimes determined whether people would live or die. My responsibilities were many, and I had units in Pleiku, Phan Rang, Cam Ranh Bay, Qui Nhon, and Nha Trang, to name a few. These responsibilities gave me the confidence to do what I have to do as head of Marriott's international operations.

The outcome of my choices—and so much else in those days—depended on my team members' confidence in me, on their readiness to follow my lead. The relationship I had with my men was complicated, but at its core, it was like any other leader–team bond. They trusted that I would live up to the Army's values as well as my own, which meant that I would confront my people and my responsibilities with honesty and fairness. They fully believed that I had their interests and safety at heart.

When I left the Army in 1972, the United States was entering a recession and the airlines weren't hiring. So I went to work for Marriott. I thought I was just marking time until an airline spot opened up. I never imagined that my job would lead to a career in which I spent more time in the air than most pilots.

I interviewed with the Marriott division that provided in-flight food for airlines. From the get-go, I knew it wasn't a good fit. So when the chance to get into military sales for the fledgling hotel division appeared, I jumped at it and was accepted into the management-training program at the Twin Bridges Marriott in Arlington, Virginia. While waiting to start management training, I worked in the security department, followed by extensive basic training in the kitchen, at the bell stand, the front desk, in the accounting department, and more.

Over the next few years I held a number of jobs in sales and reservations. I directed the development and establishment of Marriott's automated reservation system and expanded it overseas, and I opened the majority of our international sales offices.

By 1979, I was chief marketing and sales officer with the lodging organization, focused mainly on the U.S. market. But my real interest was international operations, and my mentor, Al LeFaivre, convinced me that I needed some serious line experience. Accordingly, I was named to manage the opening of the Long Island, New York, Marriott in 1983 and the Boston Marriott Copley Place Hotel in 1984.

During these years I was also absorbing Marriott's value system, which had been established by the company's founder and reinforced by Bill Marriott Jr. We truly believe, for example, that our associates are the key to our success. As a result, we strive to hire caring, dependable, and ethical people, and to create an environment that supports their growth and personal development. We reward performance and encourage cordial and productive workplace relationships. Hotel managers are regularly rated by our associates, and the managers' compensation is based in part on those reviews. An associate involved in a dispute with a manager can ask for a review by senior corporate management.

The *Marriott Way*, we call it, and our founders and their families have lived it. In the 1930s, for example, long before employee health benefits were commonplace, Bill Sr. and Alice hired a doctor to take care of their employees. Both were devout Mormons whose church and community service was widely recognized. Education was one of Bill's favorite causes, and Alice was heavily involved in the performing arts and political and charitable endeavors. To this day the company and its employees strongly support local, national, and global initiatives.

In our hotels we practice a hands on, out-from-behind-the-desk management style. Managers are constantly on the move within their properties, with no detail too small for their attention, always on the lookout for a better way to deliver our personalized service. The Marriotts, father and son, showed the way. When Bill Jr. arrives at one of our hotels, for example, he carefully inspects rooms—opening drawers, testing lamps and showers, looking under beds, making sure there are enough hangers in the closets.

Unlike his father, Bill Jr. usually lets us know when he's planning to visit a property—in his prime he could fit in as many as 10 of them in a single day—even though he was well aware that the general managers would scramble to make sure everything was as perfect as it could be. He actually travels with paint remover in his luggage to get rid of the spots of fresh paint on his clothing.

I have tried to follow Bill's lead. Such in-person visits are essential if a leader is to have a real understanding of the daily operations of his or her business. Knowledge of the front line can pay huge dividends in solving problems large and small alike.

Some years ago we were planning to convert Boston's old Custom House into time-share condominiums. One of the most attractive features would be the sweeping views of Boston Harbor from the building's upper floors. But when the Marriott Vacation Club International Division team showed Bill Jr. its budget, he found it lacking. Then he recalled his visits to the oceanfront Marriott on the Hawaiian island of Maui. The rooms facing the Pacific Ocean commanded a premium price. By applying the same approach to the Custom House, he was able to improve the financial outlook for the conversion considerably.

By the same token, Bill Jr.'s years of intimate familiarity with the operation of upscale restaurants came in handy when the company bought the Saga Corporation, a leading food-service operation, for $700 million in 1986. The purchase included some fine-dining operations, but Bill understood that these operations would require a considerable infusion of time and cash to make them successful. He sold them for $350 million.

Shortly before Bill Sr.'s death in 1985, he summed up the philosophy that had shaped his life: "A man should keep on being constructive, and do constructive things. He should take part in the things that go on in this wonderful world. He should be someone to be reckoned with. He should live life and make every day count, to the very end."

Bill Jr. chose to mark the company's 80th anniversary in 2007 by putting himself on kitchen duty at the Washington, DC, Central Kitchen, a nonprofit group that feeds the poor. Twenty-five employees donned aprons and joined him. Meanwhile, tens of thousands of Marriott employees around the world, from Atlanta, Georgia, to Thailand to Dubai, volunteered for community projects in their local communities.

Many years before that moving display of Marriott family values, I had adopted their ways as my own. Their values have provided the foundation that underpins many business, personal, and community relationships.

SETTING STANDARDS

J.W. Marriott Sr. and Bill Jr. had their own subtle and not-so-subtle ways of letting us know what kind of behavior they expected. During my first month in Boston as GM of the new 1,150-room convention hotel, the Boston Marriott at Copley Place, my team missed its catering sales target by $300,000, I thought I was in trouble. Sure that my job was at risk, I gave Brenda Shelton, my executive assistant since 1977, eyebrow-raising orders. "Chain me to the wall, Brenda," I told her. "Get out the whip. Colin's going to nail me."

Colin Nadeau was the regional vice president to whom I reported, and I was certain he would come up from his office in Washington once the numbers were out. Sure enough, after the results were released, Colin called.

"We've got a terrible problem, Ed," he said.

"You're right," I replied. "I just can't believe it."

"Bill Marriott wants me to come to Boston this afternoon," he went on.

I could feel my career slipping away.

"By the way," Colin said, "want to have dinner tonight?"

I couldn't believe my ears. A dinner invitation didn't fit my whipping scenario. I summoned up the courage to ask why Colin was coming to Boston.

"I thought you knew," he said.

It turned out that Bill Marriott Sr. was staying at another of our hotels in Boston. His wife, Alice, had been served cold clam chowder, and the general manager had not handled the situation well. The Marriott family has always taken the position that if they don't receive the best their hotels have to offer, pity the poor guests. Food must be at the proper temperature and well presented. Attention to detail is everything. The responsibility for taking care of the guest is the cardinal rule.

So that was how, according to our values, a serving of cold clam chowder trumped a $300,000 shortfall. Colin and I savored the wine we shared over dinner that night, and I sat there feeling eternally grateful that I had dodged a bullet. We made up the catering shortfall and then some the next month.

Two weeks later, the bullet found its target. Our founder was seeing doctors in Boston and the whole family had moved into the Copley Marriott—Bill Sr., Alice, their two sons, Richard and Bill Jr., plus wives and children—15 people in all. This time, all I could think to say to Brenda was, "Oh, my God. I'm dead."

For four nights, they never left the hotel. Neither did I—and neither did our food and beverage director, Marc Messina. For four nights, the food was delivered to them just the way they liked it—perfectly prepared, on time, and no mistakes. You can be sure that all the customers seated in the restaurant were extraordinarily happy as well, because to have anyone, even the founder, treated better than our guests would be unforgivable.

My reward came on the fifth night when Bill Marriott told me, "Ed, you've been taking really good care of us. But tonight we're going to go out to dinner so you don't have to worry." As it happened, Colin was back in town, and we had another fine dinner.

When we got back to the Copley Marriott, I saw Bill Marriott at the top of the escalator. He did not look happy. I stepped onto the escalator, and when I reached Bill I heard,

"Ed, I can't believe it. We changed our minds and ate in the restaurant here. My hamburger took 20 minutes to come to our table. It was overcooked."

There was no adequate explanation. I had let the first-string kitchen people off for the night to give them a break. It's fairly standard procedure for a convention-heavy hotel like the Copley Marriott to keep its top staff on the job throughout a convention or other big event, then to give them time off after the event is over. You can't maintain people at 100 percent all the time.

Bill was not mollified. "What about the customers?" he insisted.

"I'm truly sorry, Bill," I said. "It won't happen again."

Bill Jr.'s focus on Marriott's menus has become legendary. *Fortune* magazine once took note, describing his dissatisfaction with a lobster risotto he had ordered at one of our Florida hotels. The color of the dish he found "unappetizing," while the taste was simply "bad."

Our food and beverage people were dispatched to locate the problem. Their finding: The chef had decided to experiment with his own flavor enhancers, adding butternut squash and Marsala wine to the lobster-and-rice dish. The experiment had failed to live up to Bill's exacting standards, and was seen no more.

Bill Jr. worked in his parents' Hot Shoppes kitchen as a young man, which might help account for his abiding interest in the food we serve. But I suspect it's primarily just a reflection of the family's strong commitment to the Marriott Way. I must admit to feeling some sympathy for the Florida chef, having been on the receiving end of Bill's culinary displeasure myself.

In spite of the occasional snafu, which always turned into a learning experience, my career with Marriott progressed.

In 1985, I was named vice president of the Midwest region, based in Chicago. I was still new to the job when I went through a receiving line at a company event and shook hands with Bill Jr. "Hello, Ed," he said, "did you ever fix that hamburger problem at Copley before you left?"

Every time I saw Bill for the next year or two, I ate that hamburger all over again. He would not let it rest, because that insistence on getting every detail perfect was part of the value system he and his family had created for the company—the values his managers and executives were expected to live by.

Time and time again, from one position to the next, I learned that our business was about people. I also learned that the associates in our industry are the ones who make the difference. Their importance is made clear in one of the founder's values that we continue to live by today: "Take care of your associates and they will take care of the customer." And it goes without saying that taking care of customers will keep them coming back. As a result, Marriott wins numerous awards every year, including the "100 Best Companies to Work For," "One of America's Most Admired Companies" (*Fortune*), and "Best Places to Launch a Career" (*BusinessWeek*).

Values get the credit for uncommon success at another famed operation that has been family-run and owned for nearly a century. Wegmans Food Markets, based in Rochester, New York, has been bagging up good food and strong values since 1916. Today, the regional chain operates 76 stores in five states and is planning its entry into a sixth. Its consistent quality at low prices, what it calls "telepathic levels of customer service," and excellent employee benefits make competitors tremble.

The list of Wegmans' core values—caring, respect, high standards, making a difference, and empowerment—may read like typical corporate boilerplate. But virtually everyone agrees that the company isn't exaggerating when it says that its values are "not just something you see hanging on the wall. They are values our people live every day and help guide the decisions we make."

Providing uncommon support and intensive training for the Wegmans' 38,000 employees, soliciting their opinions and showing respect for their ideas, encouraging people to reach higher and empowering them to set and reach their goals without interference—all these high-minded sentiments are the day-to-day reality at Wegmans. CEO Danny Wegman describes his company's values as a way of bestowing freedom. "Once you share a common set of values, you can go and be yourself," he says.

But the company offers unusual opportunities to make "yourself" even better. For instance, Wegmans regularly sends the managers of its cheese departments on jaunts through Italy, France, and other cheese-making locales, and trips to California's Napa Valley and other grape-growing regions are designed to educate the palates of both its cheese and wine sellers. How else can a Wegmans' employee adequately advise a customer about which wine goes with one of its 400 cheeses, or which kind of cracker is best to scoop a runny brie.

"If we don't show our customers what to do with our products," Wegman told *Fortune* magazine, "they won't buy them. It's our knowledge that can help the customer. So the first pump we have to prime is our own people."

He's got a valid point, particularly in the age of Wal-Mart. Though Wegmans' commitment to its people stems from its ingrained value system, anything that sets it apart from its competitors is a huge competitive advantage. Having knowledgeable employees who are eager to share their product insights qualifies as a strategic coup and just another reason why shopping at Wegmans is an event.

Outsiders will tell you that Wegmans' commitment to its stated values is no public relations sham. *Fortune* has put the supermarket chain on its list of "100 Best Companies to Work For" every year since the rankings began in 1998. It topped the chart in 2005 and took third place in 2010.

The commitment to values does not end with employees. The grocery chain gets high marks for the help it gives to the communities in which it operates. It supports programs aimed at strengthening neighborhoods, giving young people a leg up on success, and reducing hunger. Food banks got 15 million pounds of comestibles from Wegmans in 2009, and more than 2,300 middle and high school students participate in its Work-Scholarship Connection every year. The program is designed to decrease the dropout rate and teach at-risk kids the skills they will need to get and hold a job.

Like Marriott, Wegmans' values originated with its founding family. Robert Wegman, the son and nephew, respectively, of the men who started the original fruit and vegetable business, joined the company in 1937 as a meat cutter. Upon his discharge from the Marines in 1947, he became a store manager. Then, when his uncle died in 1950, Robert moved into the president's office.

Praised as a groundbreaker for the innovations he introduced to the supermarket industry—top-quality prepared foods, in-store pharmacies, dry cleaners, and child-friendly play areas to name a few—Robert Wegman's concern for his employees was always high on his list. He was barely settled in the president's office when he began handing out rewards to his employees, starting with Christmas bonuses and followed by medical benefits and profit sharing.

Not long before Robert died in 2006 at age 87, he explained why he had been so generous to his people. "I was no different from them," he said. It was the right thing to do, and he did it. His values continue to influence Wegmans' dealings with its employees.

I freely admit that my success is, in large part, due to the terrific accomplishments of the people who have worked with me these past 40 years. Without motivated associates and executives, none of the initiatives I spearheaded would have come to fruition. They made things happen, especially when it came to operations.

In 1988 I became vice president of the Western/Pacific region, and two years later my career took a sudden and permanent turn. I was named senior vice president and managing director of International Lodging, with a mandate to create and grow a new Marriott empire abroad.

BUILDING AN EMPIRE

When we started out to build the international hotel business in the early 1990s, the economy was in a slump, and some of our people seemed to be hoping that dozens of hotels would somehow magically appear. Obviously, it didn't work that way. It took our development team years to find the right properties, negotiate the deals, and learn how to conduct business in a dozen different languages and cultures.

Those were exciting times, but my job often deprived me of an essential life ingredient: sleep. I was having dinner not long ago with my old friend Steve Weisz, president of our time-share organization, when he reminded me of a corporate staff meeting that occurred some years back. He was at headquarters in Washington, DC, and I was in Asia, joining in by telephone in the middle of my night.

Steve recalled that a couple of hours into the call, he and the others in Washington could hear me snoring. I had propped the phone beside me on a pillow in a hotel room after a long day's work made worse by jet lag, and I couldn't keep my eyes (or ears) open. Steve said he and the others at the meeting yelled "Ed" a few times to wake me up. When that failed, "we just muted you," he told me.

One value that I view as particularly important is giving our associates the chance to grow with the company by promoting from within. We nurtured that belief by setting up training programs everywhere we went. We also sought to empower our associates by pushing decision making down to the lowest level possible. I am proud to say that more than half of our managers originally came to us as hourly employees, and nearly all of our senior operations executives started out in lower-level jobs.

Some years ago, while sitting next to Bill Marriott in a London cab, I told him, straight out, that I could never have accomplished what I have without the value system that he and his father had established. It was a security blanket for me, I said, giving me the cover I needed to take an ethical path in all my dealings. I knew there would never be another time when he would wink and say something like, "Just make it happen."

Free from such pressure, I have been able to establish strong, consistent relationships with partners, associates, and guests. As the chapter-opening story about the Chinese owner suggests, holding to our principles has not always been easy, particularly in parts of the world where they are often ignored if not denigrated. The temptation to stretch the truth or overlook dishonest behavior can be very strong. But wherever you do business, whether it's in Dubuque or Dubai, your values will serve as a firm foundation upon which to create lasting bonds with your stakeholders.

BRINGING IT HOME

- *Hold the line.* The pressure to engage in behavior that belies your value system can be enormous, as my encounter with the Chinese real-estate developer testifies. By refusing to yield, we not only maintained our relationships with other owners in the city, but also strengthened our bond with the developer himself. Your firm commitment to ethical and quality standards creates a baseline for how a business connection will develop, removing uncertainties that can sour a relationship.

- *Honesty works.* Honesty is not just the best policy in business, it's also the only policy that provides any assurance that the people with whom you have relationships will be honest with you. In Germany and in Vietnam I learned the necessity of forming good relationships if I wanted my team and our mission to succeed. I also discovered that if I wanted my team to live up to my values, I had to live those values without fail.

- *Deliver the message.* There can be no letup in a leader's campaign to instill values in team members. Bill Marriott, for example, never let me forget that he had been served that damned hamburger. Each time he reminded me over the years, it was done in a joking fashion, but we both understood that the message was a serious one. Whatever my current post, he was reminding me that I was responsible for maintaining our standards of superior service. Nothing less would do.

- *Walk, don't run.* All through the history of their company, the Marriotts—father and son—practiced management by walking around. No full-time desk for them. No matter the other demands on their time, they made sure to stay in touch with the front line, making sure their properties were living up to their values and standards of customer service. Their up-close understanding of the business informed many of their decisions. Bill Jr., for instance, knew better than to try and rescue the fine-dining operations of the Saga Corporation because he knew what it would cost, and considered it a weak investment.

- *Values above all.* At Marriott as at Wegmans Food Markets, the emphasis on ethical behavior and the other elements of their value systems are integral to the organizations' successes. "Once you share a common set of values," says Danny Wegman, "you can go and be yourself." In other words, shared values underpin the whole enterprise. With them, a leader can provide the necessary training and encouragement and then trust his or her people to find their best roles in the organization. Without shared values, a company becomes mired in confusion and mistrust—a likely candidate for extinction.

- *Tap the source.* The values on which a company rises or falls originate within the hearts and minds of its leaders. For them to be firmly planted, they cannot simply be imagined and imposed—they must be buried deep in the leaders' psyches and reflected in their daily behaviors toward employees and customers, and in the guidelines they establish for their businesses. In the final analysis, the praise or blame for an organization's ethics is its leader's responsibility.

In Chapter 3, I explore another essential element of productive business relationships: mutual respect. Whatever your team members may think of you, if you don't have their respect, neither will you have the kind of connection that will make the most of their talents and capabilities. In the pages ahead, I offer suggestions for forging that connection.

Chapter 3 To Respect
Is to Inspire

We confide in our strength, without boasting of it;
we respect that of others, without fearing it.
                                —Thomas Jefferson

No worthwhile business relationship, whether with your own people or customers and partners, can endure without mutual respect. And as I've learned firsthand, showing adversaries that you regard them with admiration can resolve even violent conflicts.

The story I'm about to relate broke into violence when two grown men began wrestling with each other and fell to the carpeted floor of a hotel conference room. The brawl took place in a South American capital city where we were trying to renegotiate a management agreement with the hotel's owner. He was a volatile character, who carried a revolver on his hip and a chip on his shoulder.

The fight broke out after the owner got into a shouting match with our local attorney. The bystanders were understandably hesitant to interfere until the owner's revolver slipped from its holster and skittered across the floor. The combatants were pulled apart, but stopping the fight did nothing to resolve the dispute. After several months, Brenda Durham, our corporate lawyer for South America, Alex Stadlin, and Chuck Kelly, our executive vice president for Latin America at the time, suggested that I pay the owner a visit to patch up the relationship.

I flew to his hometown and spent two days traveling with him, visiting his businesses, dining at his club, and mingling with his friends. As we got to know each other apart from our business dealings, our mutual respect grew. Seeing him in a different light allowed me to understand the strength of his commitment to his employees, family, and community. The differences at the heart of the conflict weren't resolved, but I realized that he deserved my respect for who he was and what he had accomplished.

A week after I left, we reached an agreement with the owner. But that wasn't the end of it. One more show of respect was required: I had to participate in the final signing of the management contract. I packed my bag and returned to South America. Never risk the ship to save two cents' worth of tar.

Netflix founder and CEO Reed Hastings inspires his people by giving them uncommon freedom to make personal choices. He leaves it up to his team members to determine when they need to be working and when they can afford to play. No one monitors vacation time—though being away for more than 30 days a year requires consultation with a human resources official. Hastings also lets Netflix employees design their own compensation packages and gives them considerable leeway with their expense accounts. The only written policy is brief and to the point: "Act in Netflix's best interests."

In short, Hastings respects people's integrity and leaves them free to make their own choices. Dedicated to their work and cognizant of their responsibilities to Hastings and Netflix as a whole, the vast majority of the company's 2,000-plus employees—a quarter of whom are salaried professionals—respond as responsible corporate citizens. If an employee does overstep, peer pressure usually chastens the offender, says Allison Hopkins, vice president for human resources.

The no-policy policy evolved as a way to attract the highly sought after software engineers who keep Netflix a step ahead of its competitors. Hastings and his chief talent officer, Patricia McCord, decided to set Netflix apart by creating a culture focused on outstanding performance and without the constraints that sometimes stifle intellectual endeavor. "What keeps great people at a company is the opportunity to do great work," McCord says. "I don't want someone who's here for the stock options but isn't happy and engaged."

Netflix people receive high salaries but no bonuses or long-term incentives—although those who choose to take part of their compensation in stock options will benefit if performance improvements drive the stock price higher.

In another respect-based departure from the corporate norm, Netflix employees are also expected to manage their own development. The company views most of the available training programs as a waste of time. The best way for our people to learn, Hastings says, is to surround themselves with other smart people.

Obviously, the Netflix approach is designed for its particular environment and wouldn't work for every organization. But giving your people more freedom to fine-tune their work and vacation schedules and allowing them to devise compensation that suits their individual circumstances can go a long way toward showing them that you respect them and trust their judgment.

What does an enlightened leader get in return? Uncommon performance—because, as Hastings will attest, respect breeds responsibility and accountability. At Netflix, which delivers movies to more than 15 million subscribers via mail and video streaming, top-notch performance produced revenue of $1.67 billion in 2009, a 22 percent increase from the year before.

There is more than one way to show respect for your people, and Wegmans does it by providing perks seldom if ever seen in the grocery business. Besides its outsized pay practices, health and retirement benefits, and extensive employee training program, it promotes almost exclusively from within and helps prepare its workers for advancement by providing millions of dollars worth of tuition assistance each year. More than 24,000 Wegmans employees have received a total of $77 million in scholarships since the program was inaugurated in 1984.

This kind of employee largesse is expensive, of course, but, as the late Robert Wegman once said, "I have never given away more than I got back." The payback for Wegmans is a 6 percent turnover rate, about a third of the industry average and a huge savings in terms of finding and replacing trained employees. A study done some years ago estimated that the direct and indirect costs of replacing a supermarket cashier making $6.50 an hour ran to more than $3,600. When the entire industry is included, the turnover costs can outrun annual profits by upward of 40 percent! No wonder Robert Wegman said he always got back more than he gave away.

More than half of Wegmans' store managers started their careers with the company when they were in their teens—stocking shelves, unloading produce, and working as part-time cashiers. About a fifth of their employees have been with the company for 10 years or more and a sizable segment has reached the quarter-century mark.

As for promoting from within, Wegmans sees it as a plus all around. To begin with, when you move someone who's already in sync with the culture, you have a person who can focus on learning the specifics of the new job. Costs are less and the learning curve is faster.

When the company opened a new distribution center a few years ago, it encouraged current employees to apply for positions as truck drivers rather than offering the jobs to experienced and more expensive veterans working elsewhere. Within a matter of months, it had a crew of commercially licensed drivers who had moved up from cashier and stock positions to more lucrative jobs as long-haul truckers.

In similar fashion, the company fills new stores with experienced people from existing ones, which makes for much easier openings. When Wegmans opened its Dulles, Virginia, store and more than 15,000 shoppers poured in on the first day, its managers were incredibly busy but they handled the crowds without incident. One can only imagine what might have happened if newcomers had been in charge of the stampede. Even though it brings in experienced people, Wegmans never opens a store until it's sure everyone is ready. The company spent $5 million on training at the Dulles store to make sure everyone was fully prepared.

There may be no greater sign of the respect Wegmans has for its people than the way it approaches their ideas and suggestions. One store manager was bowled over by the handling of her analysis of a rival's loyalty program. Her boss had asked her to do the analysis, and she assumed that he would present the findings as those of the department if not as his own. She was dumbfounded when he took her findings directly to the CEO and gave her the credit.

As a private company, Wegmans doesn't release its profit numbers, but its 2009 sales rose by 7.3 percent, to $5.15 billion from $4.8 billion in 2008. Estimates put its operating margin several notches above the largest grocery chains in the United States. But spreadsheets and profit numbers can't adequately measure the value of the Wegmans ethos. The respect and camaraderie the company's values engender in the workplace are real, and they work. You need only ask one of Wegmans' dedicated employees.

No leader can long succeed without cultivating mutual respect between partners and associates. It's an essential ingredient that strengthens your relationships, and you have to earn their respect by exhibiting behavior that matches your words. Whether you're the manager of a 10-person department or the CEO of a $10 billion company, you are always on display. Your people never stop watching and weighing your actions. And if what you do contradicts what you say, people will invariably remember your bad example, not your good words. When a CEO decrees cost cutting and promptly redecorates his or her office, what message will be heard by frontline employees?

When I walk into one of our hotels, I know I have no secrets. If I order Dover sole for lunch at the Park Lane in London, an hour later someone in a Marriott across town will want to know whether the sauce had the right amount of lemon.

Everything a leader does, no matter how commonplace, has a symbolic value. For instance, when I'm visiting one of our hotels, I almost never eat a meal anywhere else in that city. If I were to dine elsewhere, the hotel staff would assume that I don't care for the food turned out by our chef and his team or, worse, that I'm not really part of their community.

Reed Hastings tells a charming story that vividly points up how a leader's show of respect can cement a bond with an employee and inspire that person to peak performance.

Early in his career Hastings arrived at work early one morning to find his CEO washing out coffee mugs in the men's room sink. Stunned to find this rather formal leader with his sleeves rolled up and scrubbing away, Hastings suddenly realized that the dirty cups were his. For a solid year he had assumed that the janitor was cleaning up after him.

"Why are you cleaning my cups?" he asked in embarrassment. "Well," the boss replied, "you're working so hard and doing so much for us, and this is the only thing I could think of that I could do for you."

Hastings was understandably moved by his CEO's humility. From that moment on, "I knew I would walk through any wall for him," he said. When a leader shows respect for an employee, it's a pretty safe bet that the employee will return the gesture a thousandfold.

Effective leaders respect the feelings of the people in their organizations. It only makes sense. If you want their respect and loyalty, then you have to give them yours. The great football coach Bill Walsh, whose cerebral approach to the game earned him the nickname the Genius and made his San Francisco 49ers the dominant pro team of the 1980s, was famous for his sensitivity—not a trait typically associated with football coaches. "We never demean a player," one of his assistants said. "We never even holler." Instead, Walsh sought out each player's individual talents and honed them to bolster the team. His reward: three Super Bowl rings.

In a business community that's ever more ethnically and racially mixed, respect means honoring cultural and religious traditions as well. If half of your call center staff was born in India or you outsource your manufacturing to Taiwan or you have a major market in Russia, you need to learn about traditions in all those cultures, from their holidays to their various ways of meeting and greeting. And the more you learn, the better you will get on. I found that out the hard way.

I've always liked to do things for myself. When I arrive at a hotel, for example, I want to carry my own bag. Early in my career, when a bellman in an Asian hotel welcomed me and reached for my luggage, I would thank him but hold on to it. A general manager finally set me straight. "Don't do that," he told me. "Let him carry your bag. You're the president, and letting him help you confers respect."

Ever since, I have let people help me at our hotels, particularly in Asia. It's my way of respecting frontline associates. It means the bellman or waiter gets to go home that night and tell his family, "I got to take care of the president today." It gives the bellman what Asians call "face."

MOTIVATING THE FRONT LINE

When we started building our business outside the United States, we initially relied on executives from the United States to run the hotels. Our rapid growth made it difficult to recruit enough experienced hoteliers in our new locations outside of Europe. In addition, we needed people who could embody the Marriott culture at our new properties and train personnel.

Even finding such people within the company wasn't particularly easy. It wasn't that our employees didn't volunteer for overseas postings; they did. But most of them had Paris or London in mind, not far-flung places where they couldn't speak the language and would have trouble finding schools for their children. However, we found a few great individuals with the spirit of adventure who have subsequently become leaders in our international organization.

In the beginning, expats made up 30 percent or more of our general managers, but we reduced that number as quickly as we could: The cost of maintaining a U.S. executive in another country was excessive, as I learned when I met a midlevel employee working in Athens for a U.S. utility company in the early 1990s. He was receiving the same salary he got in the United States, and the company was paying his taxes, tuition for his children in private, English-speaking schools, and house.

"Where do you live?" I asked. "Next door to the president of Greece," he replied. As a result of this conversation and others we clearly developed very specific guidelines for our executives.

The expense wasn't the only reason for putting our hotels in the hands of local people. Our long-standing commitment to train and bring managers up from the ranks demanded it. From Marriott's earliest days, the company preferred to promote from within. Our founders knew that if the company were to succeed, it would have to find a way to inspire and teach new associates to perform up to stringent standards. And the best way to do that was to treat them with respect, provide incentives, such as profit sharing, and give them challenges and increasing responsibility. For our associates, the prospect of one day running the hotel in which they worked isn't a pipe dream.

As Steve Jobs, Apple's presiding genius, has said, "When you hire really good people, you have to give them a piece of the business and let them run with it. My job is to take these great people we have and to push them and make them even better." I couldn't agree more.

The growth-from-within principle, which our competitors were not following at the time, was our major recruitment tool. There is nothing like it to demonstrate the respect you have for people and their potential. I told our associates— and I still tell them today—that they are the future of the company, and we are going to do everything we can to help them succeed.

The hotel business is all about service, which means it's all about motivating frontline people. I can see to it that you get a comfortable bed, but if the person at the desk hasn't made you feel welcome, or if the bellman who brings your luggage to your room pressures you for a tip, the bed won't feel quite so cozy.

A salary alone won't motivate people to deliver remarkable service. They need to feel that they belong to a service-oriented community and culture. Most important of all, they need to believe that by demonstrating their dedication, they can rise within the organization.

That was the promise we made to our associates abroad, and we kept it. Today, less than 1 percent of our general managers and regional executives are U.S. expats. The majority have come up through the local ranks.

Behind the scenes at every large hotel is a complex, unseen city. In basement areas and behind closed doors a network of corridors link the laundry with the housekeeping operation, the loading docks with the kitchen. Through these corridors the residents of the city move back and forth on their rounds—the dozens of specialists from engineers to electricians, dishwashers to waiters, accountants to dietitians. We call this hidden city the heart of the house.

The respect we show our people overseas through our promote-from-within policy is underscored in every visit I make to a Marriott property. This, too, is part of the culture established by Bill Marriott Sr. I walk all around the hotel, from the loading dock to the concierge desk in the lobby to the employee cafeteria in the heart of the house, shaking hands, asking after people's families, recalling the last time we met.

Sometimes the hotel will line up all the housekeepers or all the culinary staff for me to greet en masse. When I go down the line, I make a point of making eye contact with everyone. If for some reason I fail to make a connection, I circle back to try again. I want to do it right. Making eye contact is a sign of respect in my culture. In some cultures, of course, people will look down rather than meet my gaze. That's their way of showing respect, and I understand that.

I always enjoy touring through our properties with general managers (GM) who have come up through our training program. It's easy to see that they have an intimate understanding of the properties, easily spotting potential problems and moving rapidly to resolve them. What really excites me, though, is to watch the interaction between the GMs and the hotel associates. You can see by the way the associates smile or wave or respond to the GMs' questions just how much they respect them. It tells me that the Marriott Way is alive and well.

THE ALCHEMY OF SELF-RESPECT

When we began emphasizing local hiring and promotion, it was not universally popular with the owners of some of our hotels. In a number of countries, notably China and India, there was a feeling that an expat general manager would have more prestige than a local resident could command. Middle Eastern owners also tended to prefer expat leaders, but for the opposite reason—citizens of those countries thought hotel work was beneath them. Recently, though, in China, India, Saudi Arabia, and a few other Middle Eastern nations, we have felt pressure to hire locals so as to expand the nations' employment rolls.

The benefits of hiring locals and giving them responsibilities go well beyond expanded employment rolls. By means of some wonderful alchemy, the respect a leader gives employees is transformed into their own self-respect. It's a precious gift that never stops giving, inspiring a virtuous circle of self-esteem and proud performance. As we've witnessed at Marriott, the transfer of respect makes people feel better about themselves, which, in turn, leads them to enjoy their work and provide better service to our guests. Service jobs need not be demeaning. On the contrary, employees who feel they are respected can take pride in being a source of help for others.

One way we show respect for associates is to introduce them to business and personal acquaintances whenever possible. I might introduce a guest to an associate when entering a hotel or when stepping onto an elevator. But no matter the occasion or person being introduced, the gesture itself is a powerful sign of respect for your employees.

When Bill Marriott or our vice chairman, Bill Shaw, visits one of our properties, they are introduced to everyone from the dish room to the executive offices. Bill Marriott is accorded rock-star status in Asia, so the flash of cameras is constant whenever he visits.

We have also created a variety of reward programs to honor individual employees for their achievements—another measure of our respect. Their special talents and praiseworthy accomplishments are recognized at our everyday meetings. But our regional and global meetings of general managers is where high performance is lauded system-wide.

In the early days of the international division, our international hotels comprised less than 1 percent of our business, and their managers worked hard to command attention among the larger complement of associates. The international group of our Courtyard managers even came up with their own song that they belt out to the tune of "My Bonnie Lies Over the Ocean." They sing: "My Courtyard lies over the ocean, my Courtyard lies over the sea, my Courtyard lies over the ocean, that's where my Courtyard should be." Then some of the Americans stand up and sing, "Bring back, bring back, oh bring back my Courtyard to me, to me."

In the early days, our overseas crew's minority status made them feel as if they weren't an integral part of the larger team. The general manager sessions resembled a freshman mixer—all the international GM's standing awkwardly in the corner while a big gang of U.S. GMs talked football and cracked inside jokes. So we set up a special international meeting the day before the general session to let the global group get to know one another and strengthen their sense of being part of our organization. The bond they formed gave them greater confidence at the general session, and, gradually, as we grew, the international and U.S. teams melded together. Today they share a mutual respect because we are a global organization.

Leaders should make it their highest priority to integrate the various parts of their organizations. Success is impossible to achieve unless all departments and divisions of a company share a common culture, goals, and strategies.

HONORING YOUR PARTNERS

For more than a year, we had been negotiating a marketing agreement with the Otani family, owners of a hotel in Tokyo. The negotiations included all the cultural confusion and permutations moviegoers saw in Sofia Coppola's 2003 film, *Lost in Translation*. There were long dinners, endless discussions over the smallest details, and, gradually, the start of a warm relationship.

The year was 1992 and we had just embarked on our mission to go global. We had no plans to enter into marketing agreements anywhere in the world. But in those days, Japan seemed destined to dominate global business, and we thought that a presence in Tokyo was critical. Several years would elapse before we could establish our own property in the Japanese capital, and we hoped this agreement would give us a substantial platform there.

When we finally reached an understanding, plans were made for an appropriately impressive signing ceremony witnessed by 400 guests and followed by a lavish reception. Both Mr. Otani, the founder of the company, and Bill Marriott Jr. would attend, and the founder's son and I were to deliver speeches.

I spent days working on a speech that would express our respect for the Otani family and its achievements while also celebrating our new relationship. Then, a week before the event, the son called. Through a translator, he suggested we switch languages: He would give his speech in English, and I would give mine in Japanese.

I panicked, but I knew I could not decline. I've found that it's best in these situations to be flexible, willing to play by the other team's rules. I located a Japanese-American executive assistant at Marriott headquarters who read my speech in Japanese into a tape recorder. I then had the Japanese words transcribed into rough phonetic English and spent hours committing it to memory.

On the flight to Tokyo, I was rehearsing when a flight attendant asked what I was doing. As I explained, his face fell. My talk, he said, was in Japanese as a woman would speak the language. (Japanese is unusual in its use of so-called gendered language.) To deliver it in that form would be a serious embarrassment and, more important, it would be disrespectful to our new partners. He helped me rewrite the speech and I feverishly rehearsed in the few hours remaining before the ceremony.

As I prepared to take the podium, Bill Marriott gave me encouragement of sorts. "I thought I had done fine when I gave the speech in Polish at the opening of our Warsaw property," he said, placing a hand on my shoulder. Then he said, "What I remembered was being told after the Warsaw

talk that my pronunciation had turned some perfectly innocent Polish words into obscenities." I thanked Bill for his
encouragement.

The new Otani founder's son delivered his speech in pol-
ished English. I did the best I could in Japanese, and my
words were greeted with polite applause. I will never know
how bad it was because no one will tell me. Do I want to
know? As they say in Japan, *zenzen*—not at all.

As you've figured out by now, I believe there are few limits
on what leaders should do in the quest to remain flexible,
most particularly when you want to show respect for customers and partners. And when you are working with people
of different nationalities and cultural backgrounds, demonstrating respect for their needs and traditions is critical.

But few limits doesn't mean no limits. Sometimes the
issues have less to do with cultural differences and more
with old-fashioned business give-and-take. In those cases,
the challenge is to maintain a respectful attitude while not
yielding undeserved advantage. An experience I had in Mexico makes my point.

We were trying to negotiate additional management agreements south of the border while hanging onto those we
already had. My soon-to-be adversary was a powerful man
with connections to the president of Mexico, and a mind
of his own. He had the kind of inner strength that comes
from overcoming terrible hardship. He was proud of his relationships with major U.S. companies, including ours, and
I admired him and his achievements. But he was clearly a
tough operator.

He proved as much after we rejected his proposed site for
a Ritz-Carlton in Mexico City. A better site was available,
and we took it. Unfortunately, we completely underesti-
mated how he would deal with the rejection.

In the year that followed, small issues turned into major conflicts and seemingly smooth negotiations stalled for no apparent reason. We were left with only one conclusion: Our rejection of the man's preferred site was, in his eyes, a betrayal of our relationship, and he was doing everything he could to derail our business dealings.

Our Latin team tried everything it could to repair the breach, but to no avail. The issues grew in number and degree of severity. In hopes of demonstrating our respect for the man and restoring our relationship, I visited him several times.

I confess I was hoping to imitate one of my heroes and role models, Ronald Reagan. In the 1986 summit conference on disarmament in Reykjavik, Iceland, Reagan and the Soviet leader, Mikhail Gorbachev, came very close to an unprecedented agreement. But Reagan balked at halting research on his cherished Star Wars missile defense system, and the talks collapsed. As it turned out, however, both men were willing to make concessions that led to a successful treaty the following year.

As we talked, my adversary said that his issue was with the company. But every so often, he would turn the conversation to the Ritz-Carlton hotel site that we had rejected, confirming my suspicions that he was still angry about the decision that hadn't gone his way.

After that meeting, Bill Marriott visited the man at his office as a show of respect, and, step by baby step, meeting by awkward meeting, the conflicts were minimized to the point where we could move forward. We never again regained his total confidence, and, for our part, we felt we could never completely expect him to keep business decisions and personal feelings separate.

But in the end, relations returned to a relatively cordial state, and life went on.

WALKING (AND RUNNING AND FLYING) THE TALK

Some of our people were visiting the Indian state of Goa in 2006 when they came across a recruitment event for cruise-ship operators. Job seekers were being divided into two lines under signs that read: "Trained by Marriott" and "All others."

Relatively new in India at the time, with just three or four properties, we took the underlying sentiment as high tribute. We were already recognized as a company that was serious about preparing local people to serve in and run our hotels. Moreover, it showed our respect for our Indian associates. Giving them the training they needed to become—as we had promised—our global future.

Today, locals comprise nearly all of our overseas general managers, many of them running huge, full-service properties. In addition, 15 of our 17 area vice presidents have risen through the ranks of our international division.

We offer training in 16 different languages, ranging from the basics of the lodging business for newcomers to complex and challenging business equations for executives. What we call *Standup Training* takes place every morning in every one of our properties. For 15 minutes, the supervisor of each department talks about one subject that is specific to that hotel's mission. The schedule of the day's events is discussed, and the supervisor offers insights into how department members should go about meeting the day's challenges.

In addition to the daily sessions, we provide two kinds of basic training: Technical courses are presented in person and online to help associates learn basic skills, such as serving and control of food and beverages. Core classes prepare our people to move up to better jobs by teaching skills beyond those needed for their current assignments. Gradually the associates become proficient in the whole range of operations needed to keep a hotel running.

As we started our international launch, we noticed that managers had a tendency in the United States to cut back on core training when the economy slowed or when owners were pressuring them to reduce costs. We realized that scrimping on training would threaten our efforts to promote from within and grow our system of hotels with effective leadership. Our solution was to make core training part of every contract we signed, protecting it even in challenging times.

Thanks to the skills of Pamela Jones, our vice president for international training and organization development, our training program has become a world-class educational system that turned our 6,000 overseas managers into dedicated, motivated leaders. Most of them started as non-management associates.

In every economic climate, the program pays dividends. As with Bill Walsh and his 49ers, ours is a paradoxical goal: We strive to give our people a sense of discipline as they perform precisely defined jobs, but we also want them to be creative, able to adapt to changing situations, and willing to take initiative without fear of rebuke or humiliation. That, as Walsh himself acknowledged, is a tough balance to achieve, but it's also the ultimate in management.

My personal favorite among our training programs is, if I may be so immodest, one that I created. I take groups of senior executives on a whirlwind, 10-day tour of properties outside the United States. We spend some time in Europe, but most of the hotels are in the emerging-market nations. The "students," our senior corporate executives, do a lot of walking through the back of the house as well as the front when they visit our properties and those of our competitors.

They ask many questions and listen to the responses from regional managers and the stewards of a single hotel about the
particular problems of doing business in their part of the
world. I add my perspective by recounting past accomplishments and mistakes.

I work the team all day, every day, feed them a great dinner, and then shepherd them onto a plane to our next port of
call. If they're lucky, they grab some sleep on the flight. That
schedule makes for a grueling 10 days, which is why the
program has come to be known as the Iron Bird Tour.
Tim Sheldon, head of Global Operations Services, who has
participated in three Iron Bird Tours, refers to them as a
"boot camp education."

To give you a flavor of these trips, here's the itinerary of
a recent Iron Bird Tour of India.

The team arrived in Mumbai on November 11, 2010,
after a 16-hour flight from Washington, DC. With no time
to waste, they headed out on a tour of our four Mumbai
properties, followed by a stop at the nearly 200-year-old
Town Hall, a classical structure that houses the Asiatic
Society and its famed collection of books and coins. The
day ended with a reception that included our property
owners and their teams.

From Mumbai, they hopped around the subcontinent,
touching down in Pune, Chandigarh, Jaipur, Delhi,
Bangalore, and then back to Mumbai. At each location they
toured our hotels—18 in all—and those of our competitors.
They visited historic sites in Jaipur and Delhi, took extensive
tours of those cities as well as Bangalore, and attended the
grand opening celebration for the Mumbai Pune Marriott.
The final event was dinner in Mumbai on November 18,
after which the Iron Birds winged their way home on a late-
night flight.

My goal for those who take the Iron Bird, in addition to showing them the nuts and bolts of our operations, is to open their eyes to the cultural differences and challenges we face abroad. The tour is designed to teach our executives to appreciate the ways in which people at these properties express their respect for one another.

BRINGING IT HOME

- *It's show time.* Whether you like it or not, you are always on stage, so be careful how you play your role. The members of your team are constantly watching you, looking for clues as to what you like or dislike, who you are, and how to tell you what they think you want to hear. If you are impatient with their questions, for example, or if you refuse to listen to both sides of an issue, or if you tolerate yes-men and -women, you are likely to forfeit their respect. Without it, you can't inspire their best efforts.
- *Understand quid pro quo.* To win respect, you must show respect. In the international hotel business, that means respecting the particular customs of each nation I visit. It also means respecting each individual—from the housekeepers to the general manager, from the hotel owner to the guests. Am I suggesting that you should go out barhopping with your people every Friday night? Of course not. But this much is certain: If you hold yourself above your people, partners, and customers, you will never gain their respect. And if you won't introduce a prominent visitor to the receptionist in your lobby, you aren't showing your associate enough respect.
- *Grow from within.* Nothing better demonstrates your respect for your associates than a policy of promoting from within. In effect, it tells the person being promoted that you are confident of his or her ability to rise through the

ranks and take on increasing responsibility. At the same time, it encourages others to keep improving their performance so as to deserve promotion.

- *Make sure your people are the best people.* Growth from within isn't possible unless you provide people with the opportunities to prepare themselves for promotion, especially through a thorough, well-thought-out training program. This requires a substantial investment in terms of cash and personnel, but trying to cut corners on training undermines an inside-promotion policy. Web-based instruction can help by trimming the cost and improving the efficacy. The fact that we insist on writing training costs into our con tracts with hotel owners, thus insulating the program from cuts in hard economic times, shows just how important we think it is.

- *Cut some slack.* As Netflix has discovered, giving your people the freedom to manage some aspects of their work is a powerful way to show them respect. You're basically saying, "We understand that you folks are mature, responsible people who are perfectly capable of assuming these tasks." Of course, it requires a mutual understanding that the freedom to, say, set their own vacation schedules or devise better operating techniques will produce positive results.

Winning the respect of your partners, customers, and associates is a challenge, but a leader starts out with an advantage. Your people want to work for someone they respect, and your title suggests that you have a respectable depth of knowledge and experience. Living up to that expectation is your responsibility, but at least you have a running start.

Winning trust is a more complex and difficult task. That's the subject of Chapter 4.

Chapter 4 Trust Must Be Earned

Trust men and they will be true to you; treat them greatly, and they will show themselves great.
—Ralph Waldo Emerson

International hotels are beset by nearly every kind of emergency you can imagine. Few businesses share that unfortunate distinction, and fewer still are called to deal with the list of natural and unnatural disasters that we have faced in recent years. From hurricanes and tsunamis to earthquakes and terrorist bombings, we've seen them all. Some disasters were more difficult to handle than others, but all presented the chance to win and keep the trust of our customers, business partners, and employees.

I'll never forget that first horrific bombing in August 2003 of the JW Marriott in Jakarta, Indonesia. An early-morning phone call woke me at home, and the moment I heard the voice of Alan Orloh, our vice president of international security, I knew we were in trouble. Hearing Alan's voice at an odd hour evokes a Pavlovian response in me. But the emergency Alan went on to relate was like none I had ever encountered. The driver of a truck full of explosives had blown it to bits after being stopped by our security people just outside the hotel's lobby. As it was later determined, 12 people died and some 150 were injured.

We immediately went into crisis mode. Our first concern was for our guests and employees, and we needed to be sure we had a complete listing of their names and locations. Our second concern was for the hotel's owner and his asset; we assured him and his general manager that we would stand behind them. Numerous steps were put in place, including communications to the press and Marriott executives. We instituted a number of initiatives focused on our associates and guests, as called for by our crisis plan, which serves as our guideline in such incidents. After taking these steps I told Bill Marriott and Bill Shaw that I needed to get to Indonesia.

When a major disaster strikes, I believe a leader should respond in person—period. A phone call will not suffice. Winning trust is a complex, difficult, and time-consuming task in any case. But an emergency situation can be a make-or-break point in a relationship. If you come through when it matters most, you can often shortcut the trust-building process. Conversely, if you fail to act decisively, you may forfeit the trust you've worked so hard to build.

Alan and I spent nearly 25 hours getting to Jakarta. Along the way we were joined by Geoff Garside, our executive vice president for Asia at the time, who was based in Hong Kong. The three of us arrived on a nightmarish scene. The brute force of the explosion had blown a hole through the pavement and into the basement garage while destroying much of the hotel's facade. The truck that transported the bomb was a crumpled ball of metal in a sea of glass shards. Most macabre of all was the discovery on the hotel's fifth floor: The suicide bomber's severed head apparently arced upward like a cannonball in the microseconds following the bomb's detonation.

The hotel owner, who had been walking nearby when the bomb went off, was understandably shaken by the incident. The general manager was fortunate to still have a wife. Her driver had met her in the hotel courtyard moments before the bomb went off. As luck would have it, she had forgotten something in her suite and went back to get it. Deciding to wait for her inside, the driver was safely sipping a Pepsi when the blast hit.

Alan, Geoff, and I met with the owner and the general manager and walked through the entire hotel. It was badly damaged but, amazingly, some parts were still habitable—in fact, we stayed in the JW Marriott for several nights. We quickly got to discussing insurance coverage and repairs with an eye toward reopening within three months.

We also visited wounded guests and associates at the local hospital. My goal was to assure the guests that our first priority was their welfare. I kept our conversations serious and formal as is appropriate in such painful situations. But despite some significant and visible injuries, our guests displayed such courage that I felt more upbeat after visiting with them.

With the associates and their families, I was more relaxed and upbeat, passing along the good tidings of their friends and acquaintances at the hotel. I particularly wanted to make it clear that their jobs would be waiting when they were well enough to return. These associates were the true heroes in my eyes.

I met with the American ambassador and local officials, and held a press conference to explain how we were coping with the situation. I talked about how we were counseling the injured and those who were suffering from posttraumatic stress disorder. Finally, Alan, Geoff, and I tried to ease the fears of our associates and guests.

I never imagined that I would be back in Jakarta six years later on the same sort of mission. But, in 2009, two suicide bombers struck the Marriott once again as well as the Ritz-Carlton in nearly simultaneous attacks that killed 7 people and injured more than 50. Unfortunately, many of our associates were veterans of the 2003 bombing. I could only thank them for their continuing loyalty while sympathizing with them as they shouldered yet another enormous measure of psychic stress. When I once again assured them that we stood ready to help, and when I told our owner that we would do whatever was needed to help him reopen his hotels, it was another crucial exercise in trust building.

STAND WITH YOUR PEOPLE

Like respect, trust is essential to any productive, long-lasting business relationship, and it relies on mutual give-and-take. Each party must trust the other. That said, the ultimate responsibility for forming a strong bond of trust resides with the leader.

To earn the trust of employees, partners, and associates, leaders must be ready to stand with them through good times and bad. You have to show that you have what it takes to deal calmly and competently with a difficult situation. Coach Bill Walsh said that a leader must be resourceful and act effectively and decisively under stress. "Never panic," said the man whose 49ers took home three Vince Lombardi Super Bowl trophies. "Most coaches lose their nerve late in the game. The coach who has the nerve to stay with a program right up to the bitter end is the one who most often will have the best results."

That doesn't mean a leader is always right. Walsh actually encouraged his players to speak up when they disagreed with him and to help correct him when he made a mistake. In a heated battle with the New Orleans Saints, Walsh forgot to send in a play the team was expecting him to call. When the backup quarterback pointed out his mistake, Walsh called the play and the 49ers scored. Was Walsh embarrassed at having to be reminded? Not a bit. "We were after results," he said. "We all wanted to win."

Leaders in every kind of organization must be prepared to stay strong for their people no matter whether a threat comes from an opposing team or a suicide bomber. The principle holds true whenever and wherever your people are confronted with a significant problem.

Environmentalist and Stonyfield CEO Gary Hirshberg is a fine example of a leader who hews to a trustworthy way of life. In the course of building Stonyfield from a pint-size operation dependent on a small herd of Jersey cows to the world's largest maker of organic yogurt, Hirshberg became a staunch partner of the family farmers who supply him with organic milk. It's a hard fact that organic milk is simply more expensive to produce than conventional milk. So to encourage more farmers to make the costly and time-consuming transition to organic production, Hirshberg guaranteed them a premium price for their product—a significant cost for Stonyfield to absorb. Later, when a recession cut demand for organic milk and some farmers faced the prospect of going out of business, Hirshberg actually increased the premium. Put simply, it was the right thing to do. But it also cemented the farmers' trust in Stonyfield.

Within any organization, getting all hands to work together is largely a matter of building trust. Thanks to David Berdish, an organizational-learning manager at Ford's Visteon parts-making subsidiary, a $50 million loss became a $175 million profit a few years ago after a five-year program turned an atmosphere of chronic suspicion into one of trust. Berdish's approach included painstaking diagnosis, respectful listening, a willingness to challenge assumptions, and a commitment to showing everyone how to benefit from cooperation. For instance, when the engineers finally understood why the finance people needed projected returns and why the money minders weren't out to get them, they stopped submitting inflated budgets. As a result, the finance people stopped making automatic cuts in the engineers' budgets.

Winning your customers' trust requires a much less intimate strategy than the steps you must take to earn the trust of your partners and associates. Normally, customers bestow trust after they've used a product or service for a substantial period of time. But getting them to try your product in the first place may depend on your creativity and perseverance.

That's how Gary Hirshberg started selling his yogurt. Lacking money for a conventional marketing drive, Hirshberg and his partner, Samuel Kaymen, set out to win over one customer at a time by handing out free samples at a local supermarket. "We were sustained by zeal," Hirshberg said, "and the faith that our first client would find our yogurt melting in her mouth and spread the word to hundreds of others, who would fast become thousands and then millions."

With the help of some clever guerrilla marketing, Hirshberg's strategy worked. But his first brainstorm was just the beginning. He knew he would have to earn the trust and loyalty of his customers by making an emotional connection with them. So Stonyfield works to make its customers feel that they are part of an ongoing crusade to promote organic foods, which will protect their families and save the planet by supporting sustainable farming and protecting the environment. The company directs 10 percent of its annual profits to environmental and educational programs that promote health and ecological causes. "Since the kind of people who prize natural, healthy foods tend to resonate to those goals," Hirshberg noted, "our customers feel they are helping our cause and doing right by the planet when they pay a few cents more than our competitors charge for a container of Stonyfield yogurt."

One of the best ways to build trust among customers is to show that you trust them, advises Dov Seidman, the CEO of LRN Inc., a business culture consultant. Writing in *Bloomberg BusinessWeek*, Seidman cited a New York doughnut maker who built a thriving business by letting customers make their own change. The doughnut man saved time while also creating a stronger bond with his customers.

When the legendary rock band Radiohead released an album online and asked fans to pay whatever they wanted to download it, the album's revenues topped all previous releases, Seidman pointed out. And when the University of Michigan's health system told its doctors to apologize to patients when they made mistakes, presumably increasing the risk of lawsuits, the number of malpractice suits filed against the system actually declined.

As your customers begin to trust you, you can cement their loyalty by promptly fixing something that has gone wrong. How you handle a delayed delivery, let's say, or a product malfunction can be your moment of truth. You can either strengthen your customer bond or weaken it.

Netflix, whose low churn rate alone attests to customer satisfaction, has gathered enough plaques and commendations to plaster a wall. The 2010 American Customer Satisfaction Index ranks it number one in the e-commerce division, and it consistently tops the list of retail Web sites drawn up by ForeSee Results. It has also received high praise from *Fast Company*, the National Retail Federation, and Nielsen Online. Certainly, Netflix's technological innovations, and the people who dream them up, deserve every accolade. But it's the one-on-one personal interaction at the Netflix call center that is fascinating and instructive when it comes to building trust.

The people who man the phones are grand masters at keeping subscribers happy. Netflix customers are made to feel like close friends, the kind you'd just love to chat with at any time. And to make sure you can phone a Netflix friend 24/7, they put their toll-free number in plain sight right on the help page of Netflix.com.

Don't even try to reach a customer representative by e-mail—it's too impersonal. You can access information related to common quality and service problems on the Web site, but if you have a complaint or suggestion, the Netflix customer crew likes to speak to subscribers directly. That way, they can ask questions if they don't quite understand your problem. Nor will you find yourself in an interminable wait when you do call. With 200 customer service reps assigned to shifts throughout the day, you're likely to be connected to someone in a minute or two, not 15 or 20.

Among the other trends Netflix has chosen to buck is its call-center location. The Los Gatos, California-based company has outsourced its customer service not to Delhi or Manila, not even to the lowest-cost areas of the United States. No, it chose Hillsboro, Oregon, because Oregonians have such friendly voices and generally amiable attitudes.

Is live, onshore phone help expensive? Yes. But when the idea was presented to CEO Reed Hastings, he enthusiastically embraced it. Keeping customers happy and loyal is the top priority at Netflix. To that end, its service representatives have wide latitude when it comes to soothing customers. Bonus discs and customer credits are distributed generously. So is time—whatever amount it takes to end a call on a happy note is the amount of time Netflix wants its reps to spend.

Even if you can't devote unlimited telephone time to helping every customer solve his or her problem, you can certainly embrace the positive attitude toward customers that drives Netflix's success.

And how might you go about getting your service representatives to exhibit a positive attitude to your customers and their problems? Well, as American Express found out, happy customers are really a product of happy employees.

While perusing a copy of *Fortune* magazine that hit the newsstands in the summer of 2010, I came across this not-so-newsworthy (to me, at least) tidbit: "We've learned the importance of the attitude of the employee," said Jim Bush, AmEx's executive vice president of world service.

If you are an American Express cardholder, you may already know that the company is serious about providing great customer service. CEO Ken Chenault listed outstanding service as one of the company's top three priorities in 2010, along with growth and efficiency. And to achieve that goal, the company asked its 26,000-member call-center staff what it could do to make them happier.

Answer: more money, less rigid scheduling, and better career opportunities.

AmEx listened and acted on what its reps had to say. It also did away with a previous command to keep calls brief and tightly focused on the primary reason for the call. Now, the AmEx representatives are allowed, even encouraged, to engage customers in more substantive conversations. The result: A 10 percent increase in service margins.

As Chenault remarked, "Great service starts with the people who deliver it." And that is as true for Marriott as for any other outstanding organization. Our attention to detail and our systems manual may be crucial to our operational efficiency, but what keeps our guests coming back visit after visit is the personalized attention they receive. Associate empowerment is a key pillar of our value system at Marriott.

The stories of beyond-the-call service are legend, but here are two of my favorites:

1. A woman registered at one of our hotels was scheduled to present a major speech—the first of her career—at a national conference in the area. Soon after her arrival, she took out her laptop to make some important revisions to her script and discovered that she had left both her battery and power cord at home. When the front desk person was told about her problem, an associate was able to find a power cord that fit her machine.

   Our guest was suitably grateful and set to work on her presentation. Then the computer's hard drive crashed. With less than 24 hours remaining before she was due to take the stage, she desperately looked for help. An associate in the accounting department led her to an empty terminal and desk and helped her reconstruct her talk. He then corralled some colleagues who were just completing their shifts to provide an audience for her rehearsal. Her confidence—and her presentation—restored, she went on to deliver the best-received talk of the conference.

2. A headquarters-based sales representative for one of our Caribbean resorts spoke with a young woman who was hoping to spend her honeymoon there. When he called her back to work out the details, he learned that her schedule had abruptly, and tragically, changed. Her husband-to-be had been diagnosed with brain cancer and given just a few months to live. They were going ahead with the wedding, but much sooner than originally planned. To allow for chemotherapy, their honeymoon would have to be at a time when, as it turned out, the resort was blacked out.

   When he hung up, the sales representative was not happy. He called the general manager of the resort directly. The general manager was able to find a room—an upgrade, actually—and the woman was delighted. Within a few hours, though, she was in tears. The airline, a partner in the Marriott Miles Travel program, had no tickets available for her new time slot.

Once again, the sales representative refused to take no for an answer. He contacted another airline that was not allied with our travel program, and in short order the couple received, free of charge, first-class air tickets to the resort. The Marriott GM followed suit, providing them a free room.

Four months passed, and the sales representative received a letter from the bride thanking him for his help. Her husband, she wrote, had died, but in his final hours he had told her how much he cherished the memory of their days at the resort. The letter ended: "You'll never know what you and Marriott did for us."

COPING WITH WILMA

There is no truer moment for cementing customer trust than an emergency. A guest who is well taken care of in a time of trouble will be yours forever—and that guest's friends and family will hear about it, too.

In late October 2005, the National Hurricane Center was predicting that Hurricane Wilma was on course to slam Mexico's Yucatan Peninsula. We had three properties there. We had to make a decision either to tell hundreds of guests to interrupt their vacations and fly home or wait to see if the storm weakened or changed course over the next day.

Our crisis team and I gave the managers of the three hotels specific instructions: Urge guests to get on the earliest possible flight out of Cancun. Figuring that not everyone would comply, we devised a fallback position for keeping the approximately 150 holdouts safe.

We always knew that a deadly hurricane would threaten the peninsula one day. So our three properties had joined together to arrange a contingency lease with two safely situated Cancun hotels. We had refurbished and staffed the hotels to make them ready for our guests. The accommodations were nothing fancy, but each location had a physician on-site as well as food, a security team, and medical supplies. As Wilma bore down on Cancun, we were moving our remaining guests to the inland locations.

The weather forecasters had classified Wilma as a monster, Category 5 storm, and they were right. They also nailed her course. Wilma roared through Cancun with gusts of up to 155 miles an hour, uprooting trees, shattering windows, shearing roofs off buildings, and shutting down the airports. The storm was expected to last 8 hours, but it hovered over Cancun for an unbelievable 36 hours. It was the most intense storm ever recorded in the Caribbean basin, and, tragically, 63 people lost their lives.

After the storm passed, we had more decisions to make. Two days hunkered down in the inland hotels had put our guests in a less-than-festive frame of mind, even though we had one of our Casa Magna associates, Edwin Rios, play the guitar and entertaining the guests. We also provided food prepared by our Chef Richard Sylvester and medical services provided by Dr. Leticia Zapata. Getting our guests home became our goal—and how to do it became our problem.

No commercial flights were taking off from the main Cancun airport. Thousands of stranded tourists were milling about the terminal, yelling into their cell phones and getting angrier by the minute. Dropping off our guests to join the crowd didn't seem like the right solution—and it certainly wouldn't foster trust.

Having tried in vain to secure U.S.-based aircraft, I contacted Alex Stadlin in Mexico City. I told Alex, former Marriott vice president for Mexico, "to get us Mexicana or Aeromexico planes" (Mexicana and Aeromexico are the country's national airline). We discussed the importance of getting these aircraft and our guests safely home.

Tapping his network of relationships, Alex got us two Airbus 320s. The Mexicana planes were dispatched to Merida Airport, and we arranged for buses to carry our guests to the planes. Worried about the civil unrest that flared in Wilma's wake, we put armed guards on the buses. Happy to be going anywhere other than their makeshift accommodations, the guests withstood a 230-mile journey that was marked by downed trees, flooding, and almost 16 hours to get to the airport. The two-hour flight to Atlanta passed in a rush of relief.

Our associates dealt with a number of incidents, including a near fatal heart attack of a guest and accommodating in their home a guest who was unable to make the flight due to a medical condition. In all, due to the valiant efforts of the associates, all of our guests ultimately made it home. Our attention then turned to our associates, and our GMs, led by Chris Calabrese, and their teams of associates focused on helping families repair their homes and address the devastating effects of Hurricane Wilma.

When our team finally managed to fly into Cancun 48 hours later on a chartered plane, I saw stranded tourists by the hundreds still lined up outside the airport. Rescue aircraft were just then beginning to land. Our response to Wilma was expensive, of course, but it was well worth the money. No other hotel chain flew people out. What we did was the trustworthy thing to do. We wanted our guests to know that we would take care of them, no matter what.

When a problem threatens your relationship with your customers, don't even think about a minimal response. It doesn't take much to lose a customer's trust.

Some of the guests later produced a video and sent it to the Marriott associates as a tribute. Others sent a large poster signed by those who endured Wilma together. One family wrote from their home in Scottsdale, Arizona, "All of the employees who stayed with us in the shelter not only took extraordinary care using professionalism, understanding and courtesy . . . but they also saved our lives."

A FORTIFIED RELATIONSHIP

Another terrorist bombing, the most devastating I've ever encountered, brought me to Pakistan on the evening of September 22, 2008. Our guards at the Islamabad Marriott Hotel in the Pakistani capital had stopped a truck loaded with explosives before it could reach the hotel. But after an exchange of gunfire, the suicide bomber hit the detonator. As usual, the terrorists succeeded in killing and maiming mostly their own countrymen. Of the 57 people dead and the 266 injured, only 20 were foreign nationals.

The explosion left a crater 60 feet wide and 20 feet deep, and a subsequent gas leak ignited and fed a fire that spread through two-thirds of the 258-room hotel.

The attack also left a hole in the life of the city. Just minutes from the National Assembly and the prime minister's residence, the Islamabad Marriott was a well-known refuge for journalists, diplomats, government officials, and military personnel. They traded news and conjecture in the hotel's cafés and lounges, while television networks set up broadcasting equipment on the roof. In fact, leading Pakistani government figures had been scheduled to have dinner in the hotel restaurant on the night of the bombing. Luckily, the dinner had been switched to the prime minister's home at the last minute.

I was distressed and dismayed by the damage and loss of lives, of course, and I also felt great sympathy for the owner. I had known and worked with Sadruddin Hashwani, who I'm proud to count as a business friend, for 20 years. This is a unique franchise in the Marriott system.

I flew to Islamabad, accompanied once again by Alan Orlob and Geoff Garside, arriving within 48 hours of the blast. Barred from the hospital for security reasons, Alan, Geoff, and I walked through the smoking ruins, letting people see that we were there, on the scene, doing whatever we could to help. We worked to shore up our relationship with the guests who were returning, but our main concerns were the associates and Mr. Hashwani. They needed our support, and we were there to give it.

We also met with the American ambassador and spent a good deal of time with our managers and many of the associates. Two more trips to the hotel while in Islamabad helped us determine the full extent of the damage and how to go about rebuilding. Obviously, we wanted to reopen as soon as possible. And, as usual in situations like this, we set up a fund—$300,000 in all—to help the families of the dead and injured associates.

As the days passed, our relationship with Mr. Hashwani grew stronger. He is a seasoned and perceptive businessman, not one to run from trouble. We shared our anger and frustration over the bombing and our concern for the victims. I promised the company's full backing, which included provisions for enhanced security consultation and engineering assistance to get the rebuilding process under way.

Today, the Islamabad Marriott is back in business. Mr. Hashwani has invested heavily in returning the hotel to its former elegance, secure in the knowledge that we care deeply about him and his enterprise. He is confident that we will stand by him if disaster strikes again. We are even working together to find additional hotel opportunities around the world. We have earned his trust.

While you have read about Marriott facing these difficult challenges, it should be made clear that there are many other types of businesses and institutions that may face the danger of global terrorism. Hotels, banks, financial centers, and so on, all have to be vigilant. Marriott's highest priority is the safety and security of its guests and associates.

A TWO-WAY SUPERHIGHWAY

Successful relationships are two-way affairs. Partners and associates must believe in the honesty and good faith of their leaders, and vice versa. Much like a successful marriage, achieving and maintaining trust in business settings is a never-ending journey, prone to minor and major adjustments along the way.

When and how trust develops between leaders and the people they lead depends on previous experiences, the personalities involved, and the nature of the work at hand. By rights, the degree of trust should correspond with actual performance, but life, as we know, is more complicated than that. Our quirks and prejudices come into play.

Alabama's Paul "Bear" Bryant, arguably the greatest coach in the history of college football, was living proof of that axiom. Throughout his long career, his conceits and eccentricities ruled the day, even as they took twists and turns that sometimes amounted to near-180-degree reversals. My father and Bryant were teammates at Alabama in the 1930s and remained close friends. As a child I would sit on Bear Bryant's lap while the two told increasingly exaggerated stories of their exploits together.

In his first years as a coach, Bryant taught the brutal, physical brand of football he had learned growing up in hardscrabble southern Arkansas. He recruited players who were "strong and dumb," he said, and then drilled them mercilessly.

When he won the head coaching job at Texas A&M University in 1954, he ran an infamous training camp in the desolate town of Junction to test his players' toughness. The thermometer regularly read 110 degrees or more, but any man who took off his helmet or asked for water was scorned as a "goddamn sissy." Luckily, nobody died, though one player came close to it, and when the team buses returned to campus, the roster had dwindled from 96 players to just 27.

It's noteworthy, however, that the 27 survivors had not only bonded with each other, they had also bonded with Bryant. They became the nucleus of a winning team, capturing the Southwest Conference championship two years later. And when the team held its 25-year reunion in 1979, Bryant was the guest of honor.

Over the years, Bryant evolved with the times. He learned to prize quickness and intelligence, and he molded his game to his players' individual talents. The coach also found ways to motivate young men with differing needs and personalities: "One player you have to shake up and get mad, but you'll break another player if you treat him like that, so you try to gentle him along, encourage him."

And Bryant came to care about the young men under his tutelage off the field as well as on. He had them write down their goals in life and promised to help them reach those goals. He encouraged them to be courteous, to write to their parents, and to keep their rooms neat. His caring even stretched to opposing players. When Kent Waldrep, a running back at Texas Christian, was paralyzed from the neck down in a game against Alabama in 1975, Bryant called or wrote him every day for three months. Inspired by Bear, Waldrep vowed to walk again—and he did.

Bryant's methods won him trust and loyalty from all corners. By the end of his long career, he was the face of college football, the winningest coach in history who was genuinely loved by his players and revered by fans everywhere. Bear's story reinforces my conviction that a strong character is the key to inspiring trust.

Sometimes trust is lost through no fault of the person currently in charge. Nevertheless, the current leader has to convince people that he or she is worthy of their trust. That was one of the big challenges facing Alan Mulally when he took over as CEO at the Ford Motor Company.

Like America's other two Big Three car companies, Ford was in dire straits when Mulally arrived in 2006, brought low by the same catalog of model mistakes and management missteps that left General Motors and Chrysler begging for a government bailout a few years later. Critics inside and outside of Ford groused that Mulally wasn't a "car guy," as Bill Saporito wrote in *Time* magazine. And that was true. The aeronautical engineer had spent 37 years at Boeing making airplanes like the 777 jetliner, the development of which he oversaw. But the carping was also irrelevant, given that the "car guys" had been in the driver's seat when GM and Chrysler drove off a cliff.

If there was a bright side to the Great Recession, it was the leverage it gave to leaders like Alan Mulally to rid their companies of debilitating management practices. With the support of Chairman William Clay Ford, Mulally broke up internal cabals intent on sabotaging the new guy's efforts. He opened up processes and demanded that information be shared across the executive ranks, while also instituting a helping-hand approach among his managers. Mulally also made deals with the United Auto Workers to bring labor costs down, thus helping to ensure that the company would survive and prosper.

What really set Ford apart from its U.S. competitors was its desire to avoid a government bailout and the federal oversight that would accompany it, while also escaping the stigma of bankruptcy. Under Mulally's guidance, Henry Ford's namesake has achieved its near-term goals and then some. Customers have been impressed by Mulally's gutsy, go-it-alone approach, and now the automaker's earnings are showing it: Second-quarter 2010 pretax operating profit totaled $2.9 billion versus a $424 million loss in the year-earlier quarter. Meanwhile, Ford's market share has risen to 17.5 percent, a 1.4-point increase.

If Ford seems to be cruising these days, it's because the enthusiastic and indefatigable Mulally has won back the trust of his customers, his suppliers, and his managers. The CEO's not so secret weapon is a strategy known as One Ford, which basically means producing a single car model that will be sold in all markets. In the past, Ford and its American rivals made multiple and costly changes in their car models to appeal to customer preferences around the world. But Mulally, his eye firmly fixed on the global economy, believes that car buyers everywhere want the same thing: fuel efficiency, great design, high quality, and safety features. By building those identical characteristics into every Ford, Mulally is convinced he can attract more customers while lowering production costs by as much as 20 percent.

The Ford Focus is the first car built entirely according to Mulally's One Ford strategy. All but about 15 percent of its parts will be common in all markets. If the new, simplified design approach works, Mulally will have changed the very definition of a Ford automobile. Like renowned Italian and German cars, every Ford will have a distinctive feel as the driver steers into a curve or brakes to avoid a collision.

Without seeing its nameplate, you'll know it's a Ford when you slide behind the wheel.

Having regained the trust of his multiple constituencies, Mulally has reason to imagine that you'll want to buy his Fords even without a hefty discount. Quality, after all, is a universally attractive selling point.

I have always been a great admirer of another strong character, Ronald Reagan. His leadership style is, to my mind, worth emulating. Reagan surrounded himself with people he trusted and freed them to do what they did best. I have to admit that I came late to that practice, but at least I got there.

I started out as a micromanager, unwilling to trust anyone to get a job done the way I wanted it done. My eyes were opened by Al LeFaivre, who was then our head of marketing and sales in the 1970s. I noticed that Al gave his people a lot of latitude. "Why?" I wanted to know.

"You've got to understand what you can't do and let other people do it for you," he told me. "And then you've got to be there to back them up."

Suddenly, I got it: Even if I were the best at everything, which I certainly wasn't, there wouldn't be time enough in the day for me to do it all. And if I tried, I would simply be standing in the way instead of helping people grow. Ever since, I try hard every day to follow Al's (and Reagan's) example.

Don't get me wrong. I don't start out naively trusting that someone will do a good job. I keep tabs on what's going on—as Reagan so memorably advised, "Trust, but verify." I make suggestions when I think they're needed. I give new colleagues plenty of time to prove themselves; you might say that I'm impatient for results but patient with people. Eventually, though, I either trust a person or I don't. When I do, any micromanaging ceases. Please don't confuse loyalty and trust. Trust is doing the right thing and letting me know in advance if there's a problem.

Like anyone in a leadership position, I have some special requirements for those who seek my trust. For example, I met recently with a newly promoted international executive whose impressive activities caught my attention. Within minutes, I could see that he was intelligent and a good communicator, but he also seemed deferential, quick to clam up when I or anyone else in authority spoke. And although I had repeatedly asked him to call me Ed, he couldn't stop addressing me as "Mr. Fuller."

I'm well aware that, in many cultures, it's considered a sign of disrespect to do anything other than listen politely while someone of higher rank is speaking. I finally told the young man, however, that our working relationship demanded candor, not formality. The next time we talked, I explained, we would probably be in different time zones using cell phones or a Skype connection. I needed to be able to trust him to present an issue or problem accurately and succinctly, and then to tell me precisely what he wanted to do or wanted me to do. I couldn't make the right decision, I said, unless I could be totally confident that he was sharing his full and honest opinion about the situation.

He got the point. He finally started calling me Ed—and I left town feeling confident that he could communicate openly with me.

At Netflix, rules are few and truth-telling is encouraged. Reed Hastings, who expects his extremely talented group of "adults" to exhibit the enormous confidence he invests in them, prizes the type of employee who's not afraid to stand up and say, "That's a bad idea."

Not surprisingly, Hastings' appreciation for candor also tends to promote transparency. There is no propensity within the company to tightly guard information in hopes of gaining preeminence. Metrics, strategy, and objectives are shared in regular face-to-face meetings and via phone, text, and e-mail, allowing people to join the conversation wherever they may be. As Hastings well knows, imagination is the lifeblood of a company like Netflix, and it is hardly confined to a designated workplace. Indeed, the best ideas often emerge in the least likely of places.

Hastings isn't a desk lover, preferring to carry his laptop wherever he goes and responding to events on the move. As Hastings told Professor Robert J. Grossman, writing in *HR* magazine, creative types "thrive on freedom." Guided by that understanding, Netflix prefers to put its trust in people rather than relying on a book of rules.

Distance does require an extra degree of trust. Years ago, we had a wonderful general manager in Asia who fudged his expense account. The sum involved was just $300, but I had to fire him. Why? Everyone in the hotel knew what the man was up to because he had his assistant handle some of the arrangements. If I hadn't fired him, the whole staff would have been tempted to follow his lead.

What is more (and more important), I felt I could no longer trust the fellow. I liked him as a person and admired his skills as a hotel manager, but I couldn't count on him to give me an honest accounting of the situation from afar.

My decision had an unexpected benefit: It impressed the owner. "I never thought you'd deal with it," he admitted. He now fully trusts us to do what's right.

BRINGING IT HOME

- *Crunch time.* Crises are the proving ground of trust, the moment of truth in business and personal relationships. People see whether you will really stand by them in difficult times. That's why my team and I never hesitate to respond with empathy and whatever concrete assistance we can provide when disasters, large and small, natural or otherwise, strike. A leader can send no more powerful message than to provide support in a crisis. It is the ultimate trust builder.

- *Take responsibility.* There are crises, and then there are plain old problems—shipments that don't arrive, Web servers that crash, sales goals that go unmet. Whatever the category, successful and trusted leaders don't blame other people; they take responsibility and make sure the problems don't arise again.

Do you automatically look for someone to blame? Or are you the sort of leader who cares first and foremost about solving a problem and making a fair and honest assessment as to its cause? Taking charge and moving quickly to fix what's gone wrong, then making sure it doesn't happen again is the kind of behavior that makes a leader trustworthy in the eyes of employees and partners.

That same kind of grown-up response is essential in building a trusting relationship with customers. When one of your products malfunctions or a delivery is delayed, you need to make sure that your team reacts promptly and courteously, acknowledging your company's responsibility and moving to correct the problem. Companies that fail that test are destined to lose customers—and forever wonder why it happened.

- *Go slow and steady.* Strong, trusting relationships are built over time, and one of the best ways to build trust is to extend it. But no one can reward a person or organization with real confidence unless he or she has experienced a string of positive interactions with the other party. A leader must demand a high level of consistency before a trusting relationship can be formed; a single, significant misstep can ruin the effort. Witness the example of the Asian general manager who fudged his expense account. Once trust is lost—with a person, a company, or a product—it's almost impossible to restore it.

Just ask Ford and its U.S. competitors. Because they failed to respond for years to the superior design and manufacturing insights of the Japanese car makers, and to the changes in their customers' needs, their sales tanked. It took a while, but families that had bought Chevys or Dodges for generations lost their faith in the U.S. companies and turned to Toyota and Honda. Only recently have U.S. car makers begun to earn back their trust.

- *Yield responsibility.* In business, leaders show their trust by giving people extra leeway to follow their instincts. A micromanager doesn't trust people to do their jobs properly, and that's a flaw in need of correction. Watch newcomers closely until they prove worthy of your trust, and then step aside. Don't go too far, though, in case your support is needed. When my team goes into an important meeting, I offer to go along if they want me. Most often, they prefer to handle things on their own and to receive credit for a mission accomplished. That's the best of all management worlds.
- *One size does not fit all.* People are different, and leaders need to recognize that fact in the way they treat their employees. As Bear Bryant understood so well, there are levels of trust. If you consistently provide your workers with a decent wage and decent working conditions, you will earn one level. If you also make an effort to get to know your people individually, treating them with respect,

listening to and responding to their particular needs, their feelings of loyalty and trust will rise—and so will their productivity.

Values, respect, and trust are cornerstones of any business relationship. But to deal efficiently with your partners, your team members, and your customers, you must communicate, exchanging experiences and ideas that allow people to understand and work with each other. Proper communication is complex, and many leaders tend to give scant attention. I'll discuss it in detail in Chapter 5

Chapter 5 Learn to Communicate

The most important thing in communication is to hear what isn't being said.

—Peter Drucker

Attempts to build relationships between Americans and their foreign partners frequently break down over communication difficulties. One of the most memorable examples I've seen occurred when I was an Army captain in Vietnam in the late 1960s/early 1970s.

I was invited to a reception that marked a change in command of the White Horse Division, a Korean unit that was enormously important to the allied effort to defeat the North Vietnamese. The event took place at Cam Ranh Bay, one of the world's most beautiful deepwater ports. It was a congenial gathering with wartime comrades sharing a drink even though, in many cases, we didn't share a language.

At one point, the U.S. general in charge proposed a toast to the departing Korean leader. His speech was full of compliments and thanks, ending with the hope that the commander would have "a nice flight home." At that point, the Korean slammed his drink down on the table and stalked out of the room, followed by his staff.

We Americans stood looking at each other in shock and confusion. It was several hours before we learned that every Korean military man who can still draw a breath is always sent home on a transport ship. Only the dead are flown back.

It was a communication gaffe with serious consequences. Even though the general apologized profusely, relations between the two units remained chilly for many months and cooperation deteriorated.

Relationships of all sorts depend on the ability to communicate. Unless people can share information and ideas, they simply can't work together. But in spite of its singular importance, many leaders give the communication process far less attention than it deserves. As George Bernard Shaw sardonically observed, "The single biggest problem in communication is the illusion that it has taken place."

Across cultures, the opportunities for mangled communication are endless. Indeed, misunderstandings are notoriously common even among friends. Think of Britain and the United States. It's a cliché that they are "two nations divided by a common language." But, particularly in business, leaders on both sides of the Atlantic tend to barge ahead, trying to get their messages across without building the personal connections that can bridge or transcend gaps in communication.

Too often, an executive will walk into a client's or colleague's office, sit down, and start talking business. When asked, he or she will explain the brusqueness with the tired excuse that time is money—and no one, in the executive's estimation, has enough of either. Besides, these rude individuals say, making a deal or solving a problem is the goal, so what's the point of, well, not getting to the point?

The truth is that, short term and long term, establishing a personal connection can only improve your chances of clinching a deal. In the early stages of a negotiation, finding common ground beyond the business at hand paves the way for better communication. The exchange of experiences and ideas serves as a sort of dry run for the serious business to come, and if misunderstandings turn up, common ground in other areas can help defuse the damage and make room for explanations.

In most cultures, the personal touch is not just worthwhile but essential. People from other countries often find Americans' direct, all-business approach distasteful, and usually react accordingly. For them, business is all about the manner in which two parties communicate.

In any country, the office (or cubicle or workstation) of the person you're visiting typically offers cues that too many of us ignore. People love to talk about what they do and who they are, and the artifacts they put on their walls and desks can be your conversation starters.

I had a meeting with one of the owners of our hotel in Nagoya, Japan's fourth-largest city. His office was a surprise. Most Japanese business leaders work in spaces with clean, simple lines and little decoration. His office was filled with models and photographs of trains.

Taking the cue, I began by talking about trains, not the hotel. He became so absorbed in the conversation that he lost track of time and missed his flight to Tokyo. Not to be derailed, we agreed to lunch together and had a delightful time. The personal relationship we forged that day helped to smooth the way for future business dealings.

Some offices are easier to appraise than others. My own is filled with a collection of elephant statues, Thai statues, pictures I have taken of the Pyramids, King Tut's obelisk, the Taj Mahal, and a huge painting of an African elephant behind my couch. If you were trying to form a relationship with me, you would be well advised to start talking about my travels.

LISTEN HARD

Once you get anyone talking, your first priority is to really listen. Paying close attention to what the person across the table has to say is the essential key to building a solid relationship. Why? Because it demonstrates that your questions are motivated by an interest in the other person. What's more, you almost certainly will learn something.

I must confess that listening was not always one of my strong points. Sometimes I still have to force myself to pay full attention to what someone else is saying.

Listening requires patience, a virtue I have learned much about during my years in the international hotel business. For instance, you must be willing to wait for the other party to reveal what really motivates him or her before you can strike a deal that will make both of you happy.

Ted Sarandos, the content chief at Netflix, has spent months listening intently to major Hollywood studios that fear their business will crater if they allow the online movie purveyor to stream feature films to its subscribers. That fear grew more intense in 2009 when Sarandos cut a deal with the Starz movie channel to stream Walt Disney and Sony films. The studios knew their defenses had been breached, and Sarandos set out to usher them into the new reality in ways that would profit both his company and theirs. But, first, he had to figure out what piece of the current relation ship was most important to the studios.

Netflix knows that instant viewing is the next big thing for its 15 million (and growing) subscribers, and to maintain its position at the top of the movie-rental business, it needs access to the studios' digital content. To get it access at a reasonable price, Sarandos has had to convince the studios that Netflix is their bridge to the future, not their Waterloo. Video streaming isn't going to go away, he points out, and it's better to make a lucrative deal with Netflix than to pretend the world of movie and television-show distribution hasn't changed.

How lucrative might these deals be? Well, Netflix expects to pay the U.S. Postal Service $600 million for the round-trips its DVDs will make in 2010, and it would be just as happy to direct some of those dollars to the studios, Sarandos says.

After months of talking, Netflix closed streaming deals with all the major studios, some more valuable than others in terms of content and wait time before release. Warner Brothers was the first to make a deal, but only after Netflix agreed to the studio's demand that no new DVD and Blu-ray titles would be made available to subscribers for 28 days after their release. It was Sarandos' way of letting the film studios know that Netflix wasn't out to harm their business. The four-week blackout gave Warner and other distributors the chance to sell as many titles as possible to Wal-Mart, Best Buy, and other video retailers before they were released to Netflix.

Fox and Warner have released a number of popular television series and older movies for instant viewing, while Relativity Media and several independent filmmakers are releasing new productions directly to Netflix after their theater run ends.

What Sarandos called a "win-win all around" might never have happened had he not been willing to listen to studio executives.

Though I might have begun as a reluctant listener, I learned to change my ways by watching a master, Bill Marriott Jr., at work. He was constantly on the go, asking questions and paying close attention to the responses. In fact, sometimes he would be criticized for listening to too many people—and listening just as hard to frontline people as to senior executives. He always said that he didn't want to have his troops see him play favorites, a manager over a bellman, for example—and that he would always prefer to spend more time than necessary listening to someone in order to make the right decision.

His favorite question during his frontline visitations was, "What do you think?" It was his way of combating the tendency of employees to shy away from rocking the boat or passing on bad news to the boss.

Bill often talked about a visit he made to a hotel where the dining room hostess was receiving mediocre guest scores on her attitude. To get at the problem, Bill talked to the hotel manager, who said he didn't know about the problem. But Bill bored in, asking how much the hostess was being paid. The answer: $2 less an hour than the market rate. The manager said he needed higher-up approval to raise her pay, but he had felt awkward about asking.

From that brief interview, Bill, the complete listener, had drawn some serious conclusions: Headquarters was too intrusive in the hotel's affairs, too little interested in the needs of the hotel, and too much concerned with profits as opposed to customer service. He moved to correct matters, and the hostess's guest scores soon rose.

Bill had convinced the hotel manager to speak up and then listened hard and knowledgeably to his concerns. But to some degree—as Bill used to point out—the essential problem had been that the senior managers at headquarters had not been willing to listen.

As you may have figured out on your own, careful listening can be complicated, and it takes a good deal of time to do it well. If you rush, you may miss a critical point that can come back to bite you in subsequent dealings.

We at Marriott were delighted some years ago when the owner of a major hotel in Asia hired us to manage his property and oversee some renovations. We were less enthusiastic when we discovered that he had some definite ideas about how the interior of the hotel should look—ideas drastically different from our own. We are quite particular about the interior design of our hotels and insist on maintaining a well-established set of standards. We clearly needed to change the owner's mind.

But getting to the crux of a matter is not so simple in parts of the world where the U.S. taste for plain speaking is, well, foreign. Mutual understanding is a challenge. People from Asian cultures tend to prize harmonious encounters, and their politeness can make it difficult for them to express a contradictory position. Any serious negotiation can fall victim to a failure of communication.

Our people struggled through several awkward sessions with the owner. They explained that we maintained certain aesthetic and practical standards that had to be met on any project displaying our nameplate. Our insistence on using durable materials, for instance, and the use of certain colors turned into points of contention. He would suggest changes that were at odds with those standards. But when I learned that he was insisting on choosing the staff's uniforms, I knew we had a problem.

We had no regional offices in those early days, so the vice president in charge of interior design, Glenn Wilson, and I had to meet with the owner to avoid a worsening conflict. Glenn has the skill to assess what the underlying issues are and find the right business and design solutions; she's always an important ally to have! We booked a flight to Asia.

We had several sessions with the owner and tried to gain a clear understanding of the underlying issues. Not wholly ignorant of the Asian way of doing business, we had previously planted the seeds of a relationship with the man. I tried to grow that sprout by asking about his career, his outside interests, and his family. It was obvious that I was listening carefully to what he said.

Eventually, I was able to ascertain his major concern, which was the hotel's Chinese restaurant and public spaces and the impact their redesign would have on his status in the community. Once I knew what he really wanted, we were able to resolve our differences and reach a consensus that both of us could live with. The owner was given responsibility for the design of the restaurant and lobby, and the rest of the hotel was left to Marriott. Mission accomplished—but only after some serious listening.

Some smart leaders build their entire business on friendly conversation. The leaders at Zappos, for example, welcome the chance to interact with customers. In sharp contrast to companies that do everything they can to prevent customers from reaching them by phone, the online shoe and clothing retailer lists its call center's number on every page of its Web site. A customer's call isn't a nuisance or an expense, says Zappos' CEO Tony Hsieh (rhymes with sleigh). "It's a branding opportunity for us," he declares, "and it gives us the opportunity to deliver great customer service in a very personal way."

The company's call-center representatives are more than order takers. They break all the conventional rules and are encouraged to express themselves, to enjoy the conversation, and to build a real relationship between company and customer. Some of their talks last for an hour—covering kids, vacations, pets, and career problems. Given that there is no script to follow, customers quickly sense that the rep really wants to help. If sore feet is the problem, the rep will connect you with a Comfort Specialist. If Zappos doesn't have the shoe you want, the representative will search at least three competitors' sites to find it. And if you are having a bad day, the sales rep might send you flowers to lift your mood.

Does the relationship building work? As the recession was beginning to slow the U.S. economy in 2008, Zappos' 8 million customers were buying $1 billion worth of merchandise, a 20 percent increase from 2007. And the company could boast a healthy 5 percent profit margin. The following year, 2009, Amazon paid $847 million in cash and stock to acquire Zappos, promising to run it as an independent company with its culture and customs intact.

When Captain D. Michael Abrashoff took over command of the guided missile destroyer USS *Benfold* in 2000, the ship was one of the Navy's most dysfunctional. He was determined to turn *Benfold* around, but he had little time—just two months before the ship was to be deployed to the Middle East. To achieve his goal he realized that he would have to win the wholehearted support of his sailors, and to do it fast.

His solution: He listened.

Every day, he scheduled one-on-one interviews with five crew members. He started by asking why they joined the Navy and how they saw their futures. In that way he quickly gained some sense of who his people were. Many had chosen the navy as an alternative to college studies, which they couldn't afford. Others were leaving behind problems like drugs and gang wars. They were united in their determination to improve themselves and get ahead in the world.

Then Abrashoff moved to questions about *Benfold*. What did the sailors enjoy most about being aboard? What did they enjoy least? How would they change things?

Abrashoff listened with great care, learning details that would help him in the days ahead. And by his attention to their responses, he made it clear to his crew that he was seriously interested in their suggestions. He was committed to making *Benfold* the best ship in the navy, he told them, and he looked upon them as essential to that goal—working together, he promised, captain and crew could accomplish much together.

Eventually his promises came to pass. A few months later, *Benfold* won the Spokane Trophy, one of the most coveted performance awards in the U.S. Navy. By making an occasion to listen to his crew and gain their respect and trust, Abrashoff had turned his ship into a winner.

By the way, as Abrashoff demonstrated, words are not the only way of connecting with your frontline people. Early on, he established a Sunday afternoon cookout for the whole crew on *Benfold's* flight deck. He soon noticed that when the officers arrived, they ignored the long line of sailors on the lower deck waiting their turn at the food and went right up to the upper deck to eat.

One Sunday, Abrashoff arrived at the cookout and took his place at the end of the line of sailors, chatting with those ahead of him and behind. When his officers saw what was happening, they assumed he didn't understand the proper protocol and dispatched the supply officer to set him straight.

"Captain," he said, "you go to the head of the line."

"That's okay," Abrashoff assured him, and then proceeded to wait his turn, pick up his food, and eat with the sailors on the lower deck.

The following Sunday, the ship's officers attending the cookout took their place at the end of the line of sailors. After getting their food, the officers ate and talked with the sailors.

The protocol had been upended, the officers were talking with and listening to the sailors—and Abrashoff had not had to say a single word to any of them.

There are few companies that listen harder to their people than HTC, the mobile phone manufacturer based in Taiwan. At its innovation center, called Magic Labs, an eclectic group of 60 magicians—graphic designers, software writers, electrical and mechanical engineers—is supposed to dream up hordes of ideas for improving HTC products, and to do it cheaply and fast. The major idea-generation approach is brainstorming, with many sessions scheduled in the course of a day. Most of the ideas the magicians produce go no-where—but those that work can be worth billions of dollars.

At the brainstorming events, participants often engage in "zero learning" exercises in which they seek to cleanse their minds of what they know about a topic and approach it on an intuitive level. The resulting ideas may be boringly pedestrian or clearly off the wall, but they all receive careful and respectful attention. No idea is ridiculed.

At one point, when HTC was, as usual, looking for a more user-friendly phone, the magic labs went into a zero learning mode. Participants were told to forget whatever they knew from reading manuals or using previous models. They were to come to the problem with a truly open mind, *de novo*. From that session emerged the 3-D cube that allows customers to change programs with the turn of a finger—the big selling point of the HTC dream.

As a general manager, I held "rap sessions" with my hourly associates, a practice I continued as a regional vice president with my supervisors and managers, and as president and managing director with my regional teams and general managers. You'd be amazed what you can learn about your operations.

When companies listen hard, things go right.

WHAT CAN GO WRONG

Communication is either verbal or nonverbal. When talk is the communication medium, the ways in which conversation can misfire are infinite. For starters, each party's state of mind can affect the outcome. Say your daughter's basketball team has won the state championship or maybe you've just sailed through a tax audit. In either case, the euphoria you feel may lead you to paint a too rosy picture of your current circumstances.

Conversely, a daunting work load or a lack of sleep can make you peevish, short-tempered, and impatient concerning anything you hear from another party. I know about sleep deprivation, and I've struggled to make sure it doesn't affect my demeanor during meetings.

In the hospitality business, we have learned to be extra careful when it comes to communicating with our foreign guests. Our way of saying hello at the Marriott properties, for instance, has been the subject of many a debate. Should we adopt a standard greeting for use by the front-desk employees, a greeting that remains the same in Singapore as well as Chicago?

In the end, we decided on a different approach. We are the Marriott, not the Ritz-Carlton, and we needn't mimic its method. Rather than scripting the greeting, we opted to let our receptionists welcome guests in their own words. We believe that the personal touch is warmer and more authentic than anything we could design in our offices in Washington.

Many guests are sensitive to these verbal issues. I was on an elevator in a new hotel in Australia one day, half listening to the taped messages that announced each floor upon arrival. The two Australian women riding with me were not so pleased. "You'd think they would use an Australian voice," one complained, "not a Yank's."

Success can be the enemy of good listening. When all the world is going right, when your backlog is the highest in history and your new product is jumping off the shelves, it's hard to listen to voices of caution. The temptation is to dismiss critics as defeatists and wet blankets.

In the annals of business, one of the most famous examples of this form of hubris was Henry Ford. His achievements were legendary. He doubled his workers' pay while constantly cutting the price of his product. His Model T was sturdy and dependable, and by applying revolutionary mass-production techniques Ford was actually able to trim its cost between 1908 and 1924 from $850 to $290.

With his Model Ts jumping off the lots—more than 15 million of them were sold—Ford began to show signs of egotism run rampant. He started to pontificate on a variety of subjects he knew next to nothing about. History, he proclaimed, was "more or less bunk." And he held the same view of any opinions that differed from his own. The notion that the public might want to be able to choose a color for their autos other than Model T black, for example, was dismissed out of hand.

Alfred P. Sloan Jr. thought otherwise, and the Chevrolets he started turning out at General Motors were beginning to eat into Ford's market. Customers who were short of cash were accommodated with a loan from the General Motors Acceptance Corporation.

The Ford salespeople tried to alert the boss to the GM threat, but he ignored them. Then Ernest Kanzler, a company executive, sent Ford a letter warning that a competing product "is alarmingly absorbing the public's purchasing power." Ford responded by firing Kanzler, who was the brother-in-law of Edsel, Ford's only child.

Not until sales of the Model T tanked did Ford finally retool his plant for a new version of his Model A. He was never again able to regain the dominance of the industry he had enjoyed for so long. He had been brought low by his unwillingness to entertain views other than his own—by his refusal to listen.

For team leaders in the combative, cutthroat world of professional sports, relationships can easily disintegrate over misunderstandings fanned by the media. What counts most is the ability of a coach to communicate with each athlete in a way that suits that player's style and needs. Legendary football coach Vince Lombardi was often portrayed as a ruthless disciplinarian, berating and bullying his Green Bay Packers and doing anything to win games. "Lombardi treats us all alike—like dogs," defensive tackle Henry Jordan once remarked. But Jordan was wrong. Lombardi was a subtle man who took the measure of each player to find and instill the exact blend of confidence and fear that would bring out the best his team had to offer.

Lombardi knew he couldn't yell at his brilliant quarterback, Bart Starr, because Starr would take it as an insult to his leadership, making him less assertive and effective. But fullback Jim Taylor played his best when he was furious at Lombardi and wanted to knock someone senseless, starting with the opposing team.

"There are other coaches who know more about Xs and Os," Lombardi said, "but I've got an edge. I know more about football players than they do."

Learning as much as you can about your customers' communication preferences might give you an edge.

WATCH YOUR BODY LANGUAGE

Nonverbal communication is, in some ways, more challenging than the verbal variety. That's because so much of it is unconscious. The clothes you wear, the way you sit in your chair, the expression on your face—all convey your attitude toward others in the room or your opinion of the matter under discussion. It requires some effort for you to stop folding your arms protectively or to quit gazing out the window when someone states a view contrary to your own.

In their interactions with colleagues and associates, leaders have to be especially careful. People are always watching you for clues about your mood and attitude. There's no point in announcing what is ostensibly good news if it's immediately followed by nonverbal cues that say otherwise.

Some cultures are particularly sensitive to physical signals. In Japan, for example, your seat at a conference table reflects your rank in the room. The highest-ranking people sit not at the head but in the middle of the table with subordinates flanking in descending order. The goal in a business setting is to place people of equal rank across from each other. So your location tells you just where you stand in the estimation of your host. Message sent and received.

Actions that Americans may think are perfectly innocent can communicate extremely negative attitudes in other cultures. In Thailand, for instance, Westerners need to know that touching someone's head, child or adult, no matter how friendly the gesture, is taboo. Thais, you see, believe the head houses the soul. They also view the feet, even if recently washed, as unclean. So when you take your seat on the floor—which is where everyone sits in a Thai household—you must be careful not to extend your leg so that a foot points at another person. It's a major insult.

Many Western businesspeople try to ingratiate themselves with Thais by greeting everyone they encounter with the *wai*, the prayer-like hand gesture that is part of the culture. A complex and subtle set of rules govern the use of the *wai*, rules that most Westerners who use it accidentally violate. So, in business and formal meetings, Thais prefer to shake hands with Westerners.

When doing business with people from other cultures, I try to show respect for their customs, but I don't pretend to be an expert. A perfect *wai* or a graceful Japanese bow is difficult to pull off, so in formal meetings I'd rather not try. A smile and a handshake are almost universally acceptable or respectful acknowledgment of their gesture.

The importance of nonverbal communication became clear to me not long ago when I was looking for someone to fill a job at a Marriott in the Philippines. A promising young Filipino manager working at one of our hotels in Washington, DC, seemed the perfect candidate. I raised the possibility of promoting him at a meeting with the Filipino president of the company that owned the hotel.

"I hear what you're saying, Ed," the hotel executive told me, "but I bet you a drink that it's not going to work."

He met with the young man, and when the interview was over, we got together for that drink.

"Your man has a great resume and background," he told me, "but I win the bet. When he shook my hand, he shook it hard, like an American, instead of soft like a Filipino. If you put an American or European in the hotel as general manager," he went on, "the local people will go along with that. But if you put the Filipino candidate in, and he acts like an American, the community won't accept him."

He was right—and I picked up the check.

TALKING TO CUSTOMERS

Communicating with your customers is far different than communicating with partners and associates. Customer communication is much less intimate and the message must resonate for a longer period. But it is no less important and intricate. The messages you send must reflect and reinforce the image you want to cultivate, burning your brand into customers' minds and making them identify with it.

Steve Jobs is a master at presenting Apple's latest products, making technophiles everywhere salivate over each innovative gadget and triggering long lines outside Apple stores. For Gary Hirshberg and Stonyfield, the right message is all about healthful food, sustainable enterprise, and protecting the planet—with a dash of irreverent mischief thrown in.

When Hirshberg started out, he had no money for advertising, so he embraced guerrilla marketing. He proved to be just as adept in his own way as Steve Jobs. In one early coup, Hirshberg leaped at the chance to get some free airtime when Joe and Andy, the hosts of a Boston radio talk show, began talking about yogurt and Joe told Andy that he ought to try Stonyfield. "I'd rather eat camel manure," grumbled Andy.

Rustling up some camel manure from a local animal farm, Hirshberg drove from his headquarters just outside Manchester, New Hampshire, to Boston the next day. Talking his way into the studio, he kept offering Andy a choice between the manure and a spoonful of Stonyfield yogurt. Going along with the gag, Andy finally tasted the yogurt. After a prolonged pause, he conceded, "Okay, I admit it. This yogurt does taste better than camel manure." It amounted to a celebrity endorsement, and Joe and Andy kept harking back to the moment on the air for the next three months. Sales spiked all over the listening area—a triumph of communication for Stonyfield and at no cost beyond the gasoline for Hirshberg's trip.

As the company grew, Stonyfield's prime communication tool was the lids on its yogurt cups—now amounting to some 300 million a year. Most producers would stamp a logo on their lids and let it go at that, but Hirshberg calls the lids "mini-billboards, to be read and digested along with the customer's snack." The messages on them, which change several times a year, promote causes ranging from ending pollution to buying carbon offsets for vacation flights. Some are quizzes. One was meant for customers to send as a message to senators and representatives in Congress, telling them that "[if] you vote against the planet, I won't vote for you." A House leader told Hirshberg that 15,000 of those lids actually turned up in the mail on Capitol Hill.

BRINGING IT HOME

In this chapter I don't mean to suggest that leaders should follow any sort of hard-and-fast communication rules. Far from it. Every person you meet and every situation you encounter, whether at home or abroad, is to some degree unique and requires its own tailored approach.

But decades of experience have convinced me that the verbal and nonverbal ways a leader uses to get his or her message across—particularly across diverse cultural divides—are worth an extra thought or two. Over time, have you acquired communication habits that are counterproductive? Could you do a better job of listening to your team, your partners, and your customers?

Spend an hour or two with a team member you trust, exchanging insights about each other's communication habits. I suspect you will learn something.

In addition, consider these suggestions:

- *Find common ground.* Don't be in a rush to get down to business. The all-work approach with customers or colleagues, particularly when a meeting involves people from multiple cultures, can make for a dull and nonproductive session. Before addressing the issues at hand, engage others in conversation about topics they care about. Find out ahead of time about their hobbies and interests. It's especially effective to bring up a cause that members of the group actively support. Google their names, or talk with someone who knows them. When you walk into a person's office or workspace, look for clues. Is he or she a sports fan? A music lover? An avid reader? A parent? All around the world, people use the first moments of a business encounter to set the conversational wheels in motion. Nonbusiness chatter is the icebreaker, and it raises the level of the business communication that follows.

- *Listen actively.* If you're like me, you become impatient with too much chatter. Yet the failure to listen carefully to others is a serious mistake. Aside from showing a lack of respect, thereby damaging whatever relationship you have to begin with, the information you miss can prove costly. I find that active listening—meaning that I repeat the central points being raised—helps to keep me alert.

Also use what you hear. Like Vince Lombardi, tailor your remarks to what the other person reveals. Shape your message for the ears that are hearing it. Your acuity will be rewarded.

- *Create the listening occasion.* In the course of a day, you are not normally going to spend much time with anyone other than your staff and your major customers. If you want to find out what your front line is up to—what problems they've spotted and what new ideas are percolating there—you need to rearrange your schedule. Captain Abrashoff understood that if a leader is to tap into that source of information and inspiration, he or she has to make it happen. Bill Marriott Jr. would frequently place a phone call directly to frontline people in his company's various divisions. He wanted to let everyone know that he was accessible to people other than his immediate staff—and he wanted the input from a fresh source. Strong leaders take that kind of initiative because they know that the opportunity to listen to the crew won't happen automatically.

- *Check the cues you're sending.* Everything about you, from the words you choose to the clothing you wear to the way you sit, communicates an attitude. Using slang instead of the King's English, dressing up or down, crossing your legs at ankle or knee—every action sends a message that can be interpreted, or misinterpreted, depending on the personality, experience, and culture of your audience. Never forget that you're sending these messages, and make sure that they are in tune with your presentation and the image you wish to convey.

- *Talk to your customers.* Having a good product and marketing it well is just the beginning. You must get your customers to identify with your brand and feel good about buying from you—and that means you must communicate with them. Too many companies act like hermits, putting all sorts of roadblocks in the way of customers seeking to make contact. That kind of behavior may save money in the short term, but it's guaranteed to prove costly over time. More than ever, customers have short fuses today. So you should use every asset you have to get your message across, and keep those lines open. You don't have to be a natural showman like Steve Jobs or possessed of the imagination of Gary Hirshberg; just make it your business to let your customers know that you want to make sure they know about your product and that they're happy with it. And whatever you do, make sure the message you convey is consistent and matches your personal image and that of your brand.

As a leader, you embody your company and your brand. All eyes are on you. Both your people and your customers take their cues from you. It's an unwritten contract, but you are rightly expected to lead by example. Chapter 6 talks about how you should go about it.

Chapter 6 Lead from the Front

I don't think about risk much. . . . If you gotta go, you gotta go.

—Lillian Carter

The C-12 Sherpa transport was beginning its descent to the Baghdad airbase when the U.S. Army pilot made an announcement: "We're entering a kill zone. It's going to be a steep drop." It would be all that and more.

I was familiar with war zones, but I had only to look at the faces of my three-man team to know they were wrestling with something new and frightening. I tried to ease their fears by cracking a lame joke—even though I was batting away my own butterflies.

We landed safely, donned flak jackets, and stepped out onto the scorching tarmac. Nerves were still frayed as we climbed into the armored SUVs waiting to ferry us into Baghdad proper. It took a while before the presence of the heavily armed GIs and contract security guards convinced me that my team and I were in good hands.

It was March 2008, and we were in Baghdad at the behest of General David H. Petraeus, then commander of the multinational force in Iraq. At a Pentagon meeting with Bill Marriott Jr., the general had asked us to join in the building of a hotel in Iraq's capital city as part of the Allied effort to stabilize the country. The hotel, he said, would provide work for Iraqis and demonstrate the United States' goodwill. At the same time, it would show the world that Iraq was back in business and ready to host foreign enterprise. Last but not least, he predicted, it would be a profitable venture for Marriott International.

A good deal of reconnaissance work was needed before we could move ahead. We had to gain a full understanding of the market and the logistics of building there, and we needed assurance that our people would be safe. And as with any of our lodging facilities, the new hotel's location was critical. A top-level team would have to examine the situation firsthand—and that's how we came to be driving through the streets of Baghdad that spring.

The seasoned team included Jurgen Giesbert, a former international operations executive at Marriott, Kevin Kearney, our executive vice president for development at that time, and Alan Orlob, the vice president for security and loss prevention. I accompanied the team because I believe leaders make a tacit contract with the people they lead. The relationship, in the memorable words of Mohandas Gandhi, requires you to "be the change you wish to see."

A leader, by definition, has to be on the front line when necessary, always taking responsibility for any flak the troops get for doing the job you've set for them. That way, when you hand out an assignment, your people can be confident that you have clear and personal knowledge of what you're asking them to do. You've been there and done that.

The contract extends to all kinds of situations, not just trips into war zones. When you ask people to cut 10 percent from their budgets, or pay yet another visit to a client, or delay a pet project, they are going to be upset—but not as upset as they would be if they knew you had no idea what you were asking of them.

Major benefits await both you and the people you're leading when they recognize that you are ready to take on—or have taken on—what you are asking them to do. It's one more step in building a strong relationship with your team, and it makes their job seem easier because it's not tangled up in bad thoughts about leaders who don't know what they're talking about or who don't want to get their hands dirty. The odds of your people doing a good job increase, and their level of satisfaction upon completing the assignment is enhanced by the knowledge that you truly appreciate the difficulty of what they've accomplished. Your bonus: As long as they remain convinced of your willingness to do anything you ask of them, you won't have to take on any more of their assignments to prove yourself.

There will be times, though, when you'll have no choice. That's what happened to me when General Petraeus spoke to Bill Marriott about the hotel in Baghdad. It quickly became clear that this would not be a simple visit.

As we left the plane and climbed into the armored SUV, the lead security guard ratcheted up our anxiety when he said, "If we get hit on our way into town and I'm incapacitated, push this button." We simultaneously shifted our eyes to the red knob protruding from the floor. "It will signal a response team to come get you. The troops are about six minutes away." Then he added, "In the meantime, grab one of my weapons and just keep firing to keep anybody from getting to the car and dragging you out."

Turning to the retired Army colonel who was accompanying us, I said, "You know, in the hotel business, first impressions are critical. I'm struggling just a little with what the arrival experience might be for visitors to the Baghdad Marriott." We both laughed. Then the colonel, who was attached to the Defense Department's development group, replied dryly, "Yeah, we're working on that."

The tension was palpable as the SUV moved through the Red Zone checkpoints and entered the Green Zone. Everyone understood that the enemy could strike anywhere, any time. Even in this, the most heavily guarded area of the city, safety was not assured. Two nights earlier, two U.S. embassy staffers had been killed in a rocket attack.

We were dumbfounded to find that, for the duration of our visit, we would be staying in a portion of the huge palace once owned by Uday Hussein, Saddam's oldest son. But Uday's palace was no longer a showplace. Stripped bare in the riots and looting triggered by his father's downfall, the rooms were furnished like barracks, and the formerly manicured gardens, which our rooms overlooked, were going to seed.

For two days, we made our rounds of the city, talking with U.S. officials and looking for an appropriate site. We looked at a number of possible spots, including an existing hotel that housed a handful of reporters and a few government people. The place was relatively small and bore the scars of mortar attacks. We eliminated it because of its location, generally poor shape, and size. Frustration was setting in when we came across an extraordinary property. The site was in the middle of the city, with great views and enough acreage to provide for the necessary security arrangements: Check, check, and check.

Our team dined that night with local businesspeople and government officials, all of whom were excited about the importance of creating a world-class hotel in the city. Then we returned to the conference room of the gutted palace and reviewed everything we had learned since landing in Baghdad.

Ultimately, our findings added up to a reluctant no. As much as we wanted to raise a grand hotel in the center of this ancient city, and as much as we wanted to help the cause of rebuilding Iraq while our government worked to create a democracy there, we agreed that we could not, in good conscience, recommend opening a hotel in Baghdad at this time. We had several functional concerns, but safety was our primary worry. The city was simply too dangerous at that point. We were especially cognizant of the risks associated with bringing in staff or guests. The unease we felt made it impossible to settle on an appropriate project.

Had I not toured Baghdad with my team, I might have made a decision I would have lived to regret. But taking in every aspect of the situation, and making judgments based on first-hand information, made me absolutely certain that we were doing the right thing. As it turns out, just two years later we evaluated other projects in Iraq and we are currently evaluating another site there, as well as other parts of the Middle East.

I don't always have the luxury of observing each situation personally, of course. My staff often fills in for me—and the trips they make are seldom much fun. But the relationship we have forged enables them to go willingly in the knowledge that I would never hand off a job I wouldn't do myself if time and circumstances permitted. They've seen me wade through all sorts of tough situations over the years.

THE DEMANDS OF LEADERSHIP

I'm not unique, of course. Leading by example was precisely what Gary Hirshberg had in mind when he decided to go into business. He had been a dedicated ecologist, determined to solve the growing environmental crisis facing the Earth. But it was an uphill fight, he acknowledges, and in time he "realized that commerce is the greatest force on Earth, and that the planet's problems won't be solved until business takes a hand in the job." He set out to prove by his own example that a sustainable enterprise can also be profitable, and that a green approach to business isn't naive and impractical. "If I couldn't show there was real money to be made in curbing carbon," he says, "my cause would never reach critical mass." It was happenstance that he chose yogurt-making for his demonstration project, but the business succeeded beyond even his own expectations.

Early on, Hirshberg set out to prove that saving energy reduces costs. Stonyfield spent millions on insulation, energy-efficient boilers, sophisticated controls, and a new cold-storage facility. Over the course of a decade, Hirshberg's energy-saving efforts translated into 46 million kilowatt hours saved, netting Stonyfield an extra $1.7 million in profit. Then, to demonstrate his commitment to renewable power sources, he covered his plant's roof with an array of solar panels. Thinking the investment would take at least 12 years to become profitable, soaring oil prices pushed up the break-even point to only three years.

Hirshberg continues to lead by example, proving that Stonyfield is indeed a sustainable enterprise that returns an impressive profit. What is more, the company donates 10 percent of its profit each year to projects that benefit the planet. Whether it's replanting deforested watersheds in Oregon or building straw-bale houses in China, the projects offset enough of Stonyfield's remaining carbon emissions to turn the company into a carbon-neutral operation, the first of its kind in the United States.

My own first lesson in leadership by example came while I was a student at Boston University. I took a job as a Pinkerton guard, working the 3 to 11 PM shift at the Prudential Center, a 52-story shopping, apartment, office, and hotel complex in Boston's Back Bay.

I lucked out with one of my supervisors. Sergeant James was a muscular, rough-and-tough six-footer with an endless supply of profanities. He had left school after sixth grade, but he approved of my working my way through college. If I was behind in my class work, he'd relieve me of my usual duty patrolling outside the center and let me run the elevator so I could catch up on my reading. Otherwise, he took the job seriously and didn't believe in cutting corners.

I was patrolling on the retail plaza one night when three teenagers started clowning around near an escalator. I could see that they were bothering people. When I tried to get them to stop, they ignored me. When I pressed harder, they got aggressive. Never having been in that kind of situation, I didn't know exactly what to do. I froze.

Unbeknownst to me, Sergeant James had been taking in the action from the top of the escalator. I heard him bellow, "Jesus-f***ing-Christ, Fuller, *do* something!"

Jolted into action, I jabbed my nightstick into the stomach of the biggest kid. He doubled over while the other two stared in openmouthed surprise. In a flash, all three ran out the door.

Later, Sergeant James gave me some advice about leadership that has stayed with me. "You have to make a decision," he said. "Right or wrong, make a goddamn move. And for Christ's sake, you gotta be prepared for trouble. That way, when the shit hits, you know what to do."

To this day, when I find myself in a crisis calling for a tough decision, I often have the sense that Sergeant James is standing right beside me, shouting, "*Do something!*"

Of course, you have to have a pretty good idea of what you should do. As a leader, the choice often comes down to a matter of ethics. If you want your team to behave in an appropriate manner, you have to set the standard—you have to be the change you want to see.

Inevitably, action involves risk. During my tour of duty with the Army in Germany and Vietnam, I sometimes had to choose between standing up to superior officers or taking the safe, easy route by just following orders. In the military as in any bureaucracy, bucking the boss is not generally a good career move.

I was a captain by the time I arrived in Vietnam, and I spent all but one month of my tour in the highlands. For that month, I was assigned to substitute for a Saigon-based Navy commander on emergency leave. His post put him in charge of all shallow-draft vessels in Vietnam, including a small fleet of LSTs (landing-ship-tank) and barges. LSTs made their reputation during amphibious landings on D-Day and in other major battles of World War II. Once a week, I got to brief the logistics staff comprised of generals and defend my decisions.

I was in the Saigon office one day when I learned that an infantry brigade was in trouble in the Mekong Delta. I sent an LST to get the soldiers out. Getting to the men under attack wasn't going to be easy. The ships were sure to be a target of Vietcong gunners, and the delta waters were treacherous.

The LST captain and crew managed to make their way to the besieged brigade through a barrage of bullets, only to be told that its colonel wasn't ready to pull out. The LST had to turn around without any rescued soldiers to show for its risky mission.

When the top brass learned of the brigade's difficulties, they ordered me to send the LST back to the delta. I balked. I didn't want to send the captain and crew into harm's way on what could be another futile and deadly mission if the colonel refused rescue again. And as a leader, I didn't want my team to see me automatically doing what I was told without considering the ethical consequences.

I called on the brigadier general who commanded the stubborn colonel. "Sir," I said, "I don't want to send anybody back in there until your colonel has orders to get on my ship."

Rather than handing me my head, the general showed his mettle. He presented me with a set of signed orders to the colonel. When the LST made its second trip to the delta, the colonel had no choice but to obey, and the brigade was moved to safety.

Since my return from Vietnam, all those years ago, I have had few moments of real physical danger in the course of my work. I look on my frequent overseas travel as a routine responsibility, something that I as a leader cannot shirk because I demand the same of my team members. Though all that flying can be a bore, it's generally low risk—except when it's not.

I'll never forget a trip I made to Colombia in 2002. The mission was to explore the possibility of developing a property in Bogota and to check out a group of hotels owned by a local insurance company with an eye to converting them to the Marriott brand. Our group included our executive vice president for development in Latin America, an architect, a development lawyer, and three bankers from Philadelphia.

The commercial flight to Bogota was uneventful. I was particularly interested in penetrating that market—most Americans think of Colombia as a hotbed of drugs and danger, but Latin Americans do a huge amount of business there every day, and there was room for another hotel or two in the capital city. We met with the U.S. ambassador and some local developers, and then moved on to Medellin, Colombia's second city.

This home of the purported drug cartels, with its tree-lined streets and elegant riverfront homes, is one of the most beautiful cities I've ever seen. We had a series of meetings with the insurance company people, and then we flew in their 10-passenger private jet to look at more properties in the port city of Cartagena.

We soon decided to pass on the sites there, but we stayed to have a wonderful dinner in a restaurant in one of the ancient forts that look out over the canal to the inner harbor. At 10 o'clock or so, we boarded the private jet for a flight to Miami.

"Isn't this great?" Kevin Kearney, former executive vice president of Latin American development, asked me. "Don't you just love this kind of flying?" I had to admit that I wasn't all that fond of small planes. In the Army, as a passenger in a four-seater, I had gone through a terrifying near miss with a German military jet.

We were rolling down the runway in Cartagena, the front wheels just starting to lift off, when both tires on the left side of the aircraft exploded and burst into flames. With fire lapping at the windows and the pilots screaming "May Day" in Spanish, the plane finally came to a stop. The seven of us passengers broke through the door and began running across the tarmac through the dark, away from the aircraft, which we expected to explode at any moment.

We had just about reached the side of the runway when we found ourselves staring into the business end of a collection of rifles held by a group of young Colombian militia guarding the airport. We turned tail and raced back toward the plane and the fire trucks that were just arriving on the scene. We figured we'd be safer there.

We managed to liberate some liquor from the smoldering aircraft, and we sat in a circle on the runway 25 yards from the plane, waiting for someone to come for us, telling each other how scared we were, and trying to calm ourselves with liberal amounts of whiskey. We ended up at a hotel in Cartagena, but we were all so wound up that we never went to our rooms; we spent the whole night talking and reliving the experience.

My aerial frights have not, however, been limited to small planes. On a flight aboard a Chinese carrier's 737, for example, I watched as the copilot left the cockpit to use the restroom. When he came back, he couldn't open the cockpit door until finally the captain had to let him in—leaving the plane to its own devices.

Soon thereafter, the copilot reemerged with a screwdriver. He worked on the door, tested it a few times, and convinced the captain to leave the cockpit to come out to examine the result. The door was shut—and then neither pilot nor copilot could open it. It was probably my imagination, but I thought I felt the plane begin to waffle with no living person at the controls. After struggling unsuccessfully to open the door, the copilot ran to the rear of the plane and returned bearing an axe. The pilot and copilot began hacking at the door, finally closing the curtain as they realized the passengers were watching in horror as the drama unfolded. Nevertheless, the curtain could not mask the sounds of them hacking at the door of the cockpit. Obviously it ended on a happy note!

The most difficult challenges I have faced as a leader, though, have been on the ground—dealing with the problems and concerns of associates and partners. During my career I have believed in being straightforward and candid when counseling associates and I have faced several individuals who have merited termination. It has been the most difficult for me when I have had to deal with individuals who have been exceptional executives, but I have had to release them due to health issues or reorganization and restructuring. It is these delicate situations that can truly be the greatest challenges, especially when you've worked with someone for an extended period of time and have the highest respect for their work. My only advice is to be candid, forthright and caring in your communications. Dropping this sad and delicate assignment in someone else's lap is out of the question. Unlike the people who hired Ryan Bingham in the movie *Up in the Air,* these colleagues deserve a sympathetic, straightforward explanation of the decision, and it is my job to convince them that leaving the company is the right thing to do. In the normal course of management, a leader is called on to dismiss those who aren't performing for the benefit of their associates and the company. The most important step is to make sure that your direct reports know their shortcomings and are counseled before they reach the point where termination is the only answer. That responsibility rests with any leader.

Allison Hopkins at Netflix might empathize with the difficulty of dismissing a friend, but she believes that a competent leader has a duty to, as she puts it, "keep the house clean." Your best workers, the ones you can't afford to lose, quickly become frustrated when they see that some of their teammates aren't delivering, she says. If even one acknowledged mediocre employee were kept on staff, Netflix's remaining people would no longer feel as if they worked in a rarefied atmosphere. The uniquely successful and responsible culture that Hastings and his team have created at Netflix would be endangered.

Employees who have come to Netflix complaining about "the places [that] didn't fire people they should have fired" tell Hopkins that they chose the movie-rental company for the values it espouses, not for the money. Chief among those values is the insistence that employees act like "fully formed adults." That's the term Patricia McCord, Netflix's chief talent officer, uses to describe the kind of people Netflix seeks to hire. Fully formed adults are those who understand the business and how it brings in revenue, which, in turn, allows them to direct their talents in ways that immediately improve the company.

If, in the interview, a candidate says that he or she will "solve problems by making a policy, they're not for us," McCord declares. But if a candidate expresses interest in solving problems by talking to other people and gathering ideas that will help the business, that person is on the right track.

Technical smarts alone aren't enough to gain entry to the world of Netflix. A candidate also has to be intellectually curious, someone who has a life outside the company. Those who fail to make the grade don't last long. Netflix is in business to win—defined as the constant expansion of sales, profits, and goodwill—and employees with conflicting goals are viewed as a drag on operations, which the company simply won't tolerate.

No one is ever let go on a whim, McCord says. Two rules reign. First, employees are given direct and honest feedback in annual evaluations that cover every aspect of the job and the employee's overall competence. Managers then rank each employee using their so-called *keeper's test*: "Who would I fight hardest to keep if various members of my team came to me with the news that they were leaving to take a similar job at a competitor?" Out of about 500 salaried people, the number who fails may reach double digits in any given year, McCord says.

They are let go and line managers deliver the news, but the second rule dictates a no-fault divorce whenever possible. Netflix has no desire to strip a person of his or her dignity. Rather than harping on someone's incompetence, McCord writes the person a check, exchanging severance pay for a release from standard policies that require documentation of bad behavior and a formal firing. If Netflix is to retain its standing as a great company to work for, McCord believes people have to be able to get another great job when they leave. They usually do—and quickly, she says.

Besides taking the lead in difficult situations, leaders need to be role models for the truth telling and fair-minded critiques they expect from their followers. Business leaders cannot properly do their jobs without straight talk and honest input from those who work for them. Former Navy Captain D. Michael Abrashoff learned from Defense Secretary William Perry how to guard against yes-men and -women by never indicating which decision he favored until all the alternatives had been thoroughly debated.

But Abrashoff, who converted the dysfunctional guided missile destroyer USS *Benfold*, into the Navy's best ship, also stresses that you won't get the whole story from your employees until you make it absolutely clear that you want the facts unvarnished and will never punish bad-news messengers or colleagues who challenge your ideas.

Leading by example, Abrashoff encouraged no-holds-barred critiques of *Benfold*'s exercises; the crew was free to speak their minds. When an ordinary seaman told the captain that time and money had been wasted because "your seamanship stunk today," the sailor wasn't keelhauled.

In fact, leaders often need to check their egos. Straight talk from your people can be invaluable. I learned the importance of that prescription in the summer of 2008 when trouble between Russia and the Republic of Georgia, once a member of the Soviet Union, reached a breaking point.

Marriott has two hotels in Tbilisi, the Georgian capital, and as the saber rattling escalated, we began to fear that a Russian invasion was imminent. Both hotels were filled to capacity, primarily with journalists. We knew that an invasion was apt to trigger chaos and looting, so we posted armed guards at each property. If the situation deteriorated badly, our contingency plan dictated that we gather our guests in the hotel ballrooms, with the armed guards watching over them.

On August 8, Russian tanks rolled across the border. At Marriott's headquarters in Washington, DC, we watched

CNN and BBC and worried what the invasion would mean for our colleagues and guests in Tbilisi. Suddenly, I realized that I might have made a terrible mistake. When the Russians arrived at our hotels, how would they react to seeing armed guards? Would they be viewed as a threat and would that trigger a firefight?

I contacted the hotels with clear, pointed directions for the guards: "Put the guns down. Do not try to take on the Russian army."

As it happened, the tanks never entered Tbilisi. Our guests happily celebrated their narrow escape in the hotels' bars. My celebration was quieter, but no less elated. I was enormously grateful that my mistake had caused no harm, and that led me to consider once again the risks and responsibilities of leadership.

Yes, it is vital for leaders to be able to reach quick decisions and act firmly in a crisis. But it is just as important to be able to reverse early decisions if they prove inadequate, and to come up with new and better versions. Don't let concerns about losing face keep you from doing what needs to be done. Your colleagues, your customers, and your company cannot be held hostage to your ego.

If I had been unwilling to issue new orders and those tanks had rolled into the city and reached our hotels, I could have been responsible for the injury or death of the guards and anyone else, including our guests and associates, within range of Russian weapons. That near calamity is something I'll never forget.

My life as an executive of a global hotel chain may be miles away from the situations you encounter in your enterprise. But the ideas and approaches I've put forward in this chapter are, I believe, applicable to any leader in every kind of organization—profit or nonprofit, local, national, or international. And no matter where you put them into practice, be it an Omaha boardroom or an Afghan battlefield, your troops will appreciate your readiness to take on any job you assign to them.

BRINGING IT HOME

- *Don't skip the hard stuff.* Look back to a point in your own career when an unpleasant assignment prompted you to think, "I'd like to see *him* take on something like this." That reaction meant you started the task with a negative attitude, which reduced your chances of doing a good job. To prevent the same kind of reaction and outcome among your own people while also winning their respect, you must let them know that you have done everything you're asking them to do and stand ready to do so again.

- *Don't dither.* One of a leader's most important jobs is to make decisions. No matter how a company is organized or how empowered its front line, some decisions can only be made by the leader. And when those moments of truth arrive, you cannot afford to hesitate for long. Whatever the problem you must solve, it will only grow worse over time. Moreover, your indecisiveness may cause your team to lose faith in you. Get all the facts, and then, as Sergeant James advised me, "*Do* something!"

- *Talk straight.* There are all sorts of reasons, practical and spiritual, for leaders to speak truth to their team. High on my list is my need to hear truth spoken back to me. I cannot function effectively if my people don't tell me the bad as well as the good. Two ways to make that happen: Be honest with your team members, and don't punish the bearer of bad news. Above all, make it clear, as Mike Abrashoff did, that voicing a critical opinion *will not* be held against those who speak out.

- *Put ego aside.* Leaders need to beware of the occupational hazard called ego. Once you don the mantle of leadership, you may be sorely tempted to resist any move that might demean you in others' eyes. Be decisive, yes, but do your homework first. Be ready to do anything you ask of your troops, but don't take credit for their ideas or accomplishments. And if you see that a decision you've made is not working out, don't worry about losing face; admit your error and move on. No one expects you to be perfect—just as long as you're right roughly 90 percent of the time.

Now turn to Chapter 7 to learn how knowledge of cultural differences can save you from driving your enterprise over a cliff.

Chapter 7 The Past Lives On

The past is not dead. In fact, it's not even the past.
—William Faulkner

When I was serving in Germany, an Air Force buddy and I were intent on living up to the late 1960s bachelor ideal. And since we were stationed at Rhein-Main Air Base, close by the Frankfurt airport, we had no shortage of female flight attendants to date. My girlfriend at the time was Danish, and my buddy's girl was German.

One day, the four of us took a romantic cruise up the Rhine to the Rudesheim Wine Festival. My buddy and I were sampling a wonderful Riesling at the bar when we heard screams coming from the fountain in the courtyard. We rushed to see what all the commotion was about only to find our dates tearing at each other's hair. We were disappointed to learn that the girls weren't fighting over us. Rather, the fight erupted over a simple case of national enmity. World War II had ended more than two decades earlier, but the Danes could not forget the German occupation.

In most parts of the world, history lives on in the division between conquered peoples and those who did the conquering. Unlike the United States, most nations are not melting pots. Their populations tend to be homogeneous successive generations living in the same cities as their ancestors and remembering the same events—or, rather, the stories passed down about those events.

We at Marriott have learned that history explains the way some hotel owners and local associates interact with one another and with their guests. Given the long years of bloodshed that followed Britain's occupation of Ireland, I know not to assign a British manager to run an Irish hotel. Similarly, Japan's repeated invasions and extensive occupation of Korea over the centuries make it unwise to put a Japanese manager in a Korean hotel.

Even in the polyglot U.S. workplace, long-held national animosities can simmer just beneath the surface, ready to explode when problems arise or employees feel pressured. The more you know about your employees' backgrounds and historic conflicts—the centuries-old ethnic hatreds in the Balkans, for instance—the better prepared you will be to head off trouble before it strikes or to smooth angry feelings once they erupt.

In your dealings with people and organizations based abroad, you can avoid pitfalls by learning which nationalities still harbor ancient (and not so ancient) animosities. Not to paint with too broad a brush, but the Chinese, for example, are generally suspicious of all foreigners because of the way in which the British-backed opium trade and the subsequent Opium Wars devastated Chinese society. The discord dates to the 1830s, but the derogatory term *gweilo*, loosely translated as "foreign devil" and popularized during the Opium Wars, is still heard today. Provincial prejudices are common in China, too, and they arise with no assistance from foreigners. If you were to strike up a conversation with a Shanghai native, say, you would be wise to keep quiet about any preferences you may have for Hong Kong. Such favoritism would be taken as an insult to Shanghai.

I vividly remember the negotiations we had with a wealthy Thai family over one of the first hotels we opened in that country. As usual, there were many details to be ironed out, but our general manager reported that the discussions were cordial—until, that is, he started presenting the resumes of the people we had chosen for the key positions at the hotel. I then received a call from one of the owners who, in an uncharacteristically assertive manner, informed me that he intended to choose a Thai person for the controller position. Under the contract, that prerogative belonged to Marriott, but he was adamant. I soon realized that this was not an issue we could resolve on the telephone, and I booked a flight to Bangkok.

The first encounter with the owner was over an elaborate luncheon at which we discussed everything except the business at hand—the traditional Thai indirect approach. Once the meal was over, we settled down to talk, but I found that he was determined to have his way.

I couldn't understand why he was taking such a firm stand despite the contract, and I cast about for an explanation. Finally I asked him to answer a theoretical question: If he were to set up a new company, were there any countries from which he would not select a key executive? He quickly came up with a list of eight countries, and number two on the list was the country of origin of our candidate for controller.

I moved our discussion on to other subjects, and eventually requested 48 hours to find a solution for the controller issue. When we came up with an American candidate for the job two days later, he was immediately accepted. We could have suggested any nationality except those on his list, and we would have achieved the same result. National enmities have a long life.

Hometown pride also colors the workplace. Initially, we put Hong Kong citizens in management roles on the mainland, but pressure began to mount to replace them with locals. People from Hong Kong are seen as outsiders and not true Chinese. Nor are such preferences limited to China. I've experienced such issues from Israel to India.

Of course, the national history that each of us carries does not always produce negative feelings. Many Americans fondly remember France's contribution to our War of Independence, much as the French remember our role in liberating their country during World War II. Similarly, Australia and the United States share a close relationship borne of our joint experiences as British colonies and World War allies. Leaders can make good use of such friendly dispositions when forming and leading teams.

Knowing the history of employees and customers who hail from other countries and cultures can also be a boon to your sales efforts. It's like having an on-site tutorial about the background and workings of companies in your targeted markets. The more you know and understand about them, the easier it will be to form solid relationships based on mutual interests and free-flowing conversation.

Sadly, no amount of knowledge gathering and bridge building will erase all animosity. Historical and cultural differences will still ignite brushfires. Leaders must examine their companies' operations in that light and develop strategies to cope with potential trouble spots. Is a long-standing separatist movement near your overseas factory on the verge of exploding into violence? Or how will your people react when they learn that your new manager hails from a region long seen as backward and untrustworthy.

Years of seasoning in the global stew have taught me that having a clear understanding of the cultural and historical heritage of associates, partners, and customers can greatly improve your chances of creating close, mutually beneficial associations with them. The past still lives in ways that have an impact on the bottom line, for better and for worse. But the bricks of cultural understanding and the mortar of two-way respect—the foundation on which sound relationships are built—make for a structure not easily toppled.

DO YOUR HOMEWORK

It is almost impossible to exaggerate the importance of cultural understanding to a leader's career—and that holds true both at home and abroad. The United States, after all, is still the world's melting pot, and the tastes, desires, and behavioral standards of many employees and customers, young and old, are influenced by their home cultures. Leaders need to adjust their personnel policies, products, and services to take account of the differences. Those who do will gain an advantage.

The diversity within companies today is extraordinary. At Marriott, for example, at least 22 languages are spoken in our U.S. hotels alone. To keep abreast of the changing landscape, you must get out of your office on a regular basis and spend time with people in the field. Check in with customers and partners and actively seek ways to understand and accommodate their needs and expectations. It always helps to forge connections between people who might otherwise never meet in person. My own Iron Bird Tour gives Marriott's corporate executives the opportunity to see firsthand the countries, cities, properties, and personnel they typically deal with from long distances.

When we began building Marriott Lodging International, we adopted a policy I highly recommend: We made sure to do our cultural homework, exploring the traditions, history, and attitudes of the countries in which we hoped to open hotels. What may sound like an obvious tactic is, in my experience, a great piece of advice that is embraced mostly in the breach. I first learned that lesson in high school.

Raised as a Congregationalist, I eagerly accepted my high school girlfriend's invitation to join her for what would be my first service in a Catholic church. I didn't bother to ask her any questions about the differences between the two services. Sure enough, when the people in our pew pulled down the kneeler, I wasn't expecting it and the heavy wooden board landed on my foot. I let out a loud yelp that embarrassed her a little and me a lot.

Before I became involved in building the Marriott International division, the company had built a JW Marriott in Hong Kong. The U.S.-based team in charge, however, was operating under U.S. assumptions and paid little attention to whether the accommodations they designed would suit Asian preferences. Mistakes were made. The executive lounge, for example, was too small because none of our people knew that such lounges are hugely popular in Asia as a place to do business. Eventually, we had to eliminate some hotel rooms to make room for a larger lounge—and it's still not as big as it should be.

Similarly, the health club was too small. In many Asian markets, the clubs are much larger than we are used to in the United States because they attract such a huge number of customers. The JW Marriott in Seoul was built after the Hong Kong mistake came to the fore, and its health club and spa take up 150,000 square feet of space. We also have a golf pro on staff to satisfy Asians' passions for the game.

Early in our international explorations, we discovered that, in many foreign cultures, meals take on much greater significance than they do in the West. Hotel restaurants are a favorite site for business meetings, major events, celebrations, and simply building relationships. And to a far greater extent than in the United States, many countries make food, and the ceremony that accompanies it, a key part of strengthening connections. Lunches and dinners are a time for gaining mutual understanding and showing respect, and the quality of the food and beverages can make or break a hotel's reputation—not to mention its profit and loss statement. Food and drink often generates as much revenue as room sales.

We manage numerous hotels that have 8 to 10 restaurants. In the JW Marriott Hotel in Mumbai, 6 restaurants serve 2,500 meals a day. Extensive market research helps us to satisfy the preferences of our diverse group of customers.

Having learned some hard lessons, we were especially cautious in venturing into mainland China. Two or three years before Marriott established a presence there in 1997, we had teams visiting hotels, checking out our future competitors, and asking questions about the differences between Western and Chinese cultures and policies. The differences were many—far more, in fact, than we see today.

One incident we heard about occurred in the 1970s at a Beijing hotel run by a German company. The resident manager, an expat from Germany, had fallen in love with a Chinese woman. When the director of security got wind of the relationship, he marched into the office of the general manager and ordered him to break up the romance. The general manager could do nothing but comply because, at the time, the security agent reported to him and the secret police. The resident manager refused to stop seeing the woman and, instead, took her on a weekend trip. He was summarily deported, and she was imprisoned.

I asked a Chinese acquaintance to explain the government's reaction. "It's the purity of the race," she said, very matter-of-factly. If we had used that excuse for any action taken in the United States, we would have been pilloried. This was China, and if we wanted to do business here, we had to try to understand and accept its rules. Again, "pragmatic flexibility" was the watchword.

THE BENEFITS OF UNDERSTANDING

Companies have cultures, too, of course, and making sure that your employees know and understand your history and values can help to bind a diverse group of people into a united workforce. No one does it better than Nike, which bares its soul by, well, relating the story of how its waffled *sole* came to revolutionize athletic footwear.

Before there was a *Swoosh* logo, Air Jordans, and a towering wall of specially designed shoes to fit every sport under the sun, there were Bill Bowerman, Phil Knight, and Steve Prefontaine. Bowerman was the longtime, well-respected track and field coach at the University of Oregon. Knight was a good middle-distance runner at the school in the last half of the 1950s, and Prefontaine (known as *Pre*) was a sensational Coos Bay track star coached by Bowerman a decade later. Pre sped to a fourth-place finish in the 5,000-meter race at the 1972 Munich Olympics and broke U.S. records in seven distances, ranging from 2,000 meters to 10,000 meters. What looked to be an unrivaled running career was cut short when the 24-year-old Pre was killed in a 1975 car accident. (His galvanizing life story has been immortalized in two movies, *Prefontaine* and *Without Limits*.) These three men lie at the heart of the Nike story that has inspired and encouraged legions of employees from cashiers to salespeople and up-and-coming executives.

As the corporate Web site puts it, "When Nike breathed its first breath, it inhaled the spirit" of Bowerman and Knight, who joined hands to found the company in the mid-1960s, naming it Blue Ribbon Sports. Prefontaine entered the story a few years later when he began pressing the fledgling company, now called Nike, to constantly improve its products. Knight, who today serves as the company's chairman, calls Pre the "soul of Nike" because of his never-say-die attitude.

At the beginning, Knight, with a Stanford MBA degree in hand, sold Tiger running shoes out of the trunk of his car. Bowerman, meanwhile, was tearing the shoes apart to figure out ways to make them lighter and more durable. The archetypal tale of innovation that to this day inspires Nike employees to "just do it" concerns the birth of the company's famous waffle sole. Coach Bowerman's runners had tried various shoe designs, none of which suited the coach. So he took his wife's waffle iron out to his workshop and poured rubber into its grid. His do-it-yourself sole provided better traction with less weight. The rest, as they say, is history.

Consumers the world over may associate Nike with a long list of sports legends ranging from tennis star Ilie Nastase to the world's greatest female athlete, Jackie Joyner-Kersee, and basketball legend Michael Jordan. But Nike knows that star power comes and goes. What's important in shaping a company's future are inspirational stories from the past. Hearing about predetermined effort to find better gear for runners, for example, is really a story about Nike's promise to meet the needs of athletes. And when new hires learn that Coach Bowerman poured hot rubber into a waffle iron, they're absorbing the notion of product innovation. To that end, a crew of storytellers drawn from the ranks of Nike's senior management spends a good deal of time inculcating new employees with thrilling tales of the past. Holding tight to your heritage and values can be the anchor that keeps you from capsizing in stormy economic seas or crumbling under the weight of unfortunate mistakes. Marriott has a clear set of cultural values, which I discussed in earlier chapters. They also have distinct brand cultures and promises which complement their corporates values. This heightens the challenges of a hotel manager.

Acquainting yourself with the customs and foibles of any culture will help you avoid embarrassing and potentially damaging mistakes. Such knowledge can also guide you to the right tactic for gaining advantage.

As civil rights leader Whitney Young Jr. aptly remarked: "It is better to be prepared for an opportunity and not have one than to have an opportunity and not be prepared." The same goes for problems. Like opportunities, they generally don't announce their approaching arrival. But if you have trip wires in place, and if you have contingency plans for major areas of your operation, you are more likely to weather the storm with little if any damage.

It's crucial to remember that cultures evolve and change, and if you don't stay abreast, you can be tripped up by what you think you understand. The story of Henry Luce, founder of Time Inc. and its subsequent publishing empire, provides a cautionary tale.

Born to a missionary and his wife in China at the end of the nineteenth century, "small boy Luce," as the servants called him, remained fascinated by the country all his life. But his vision was fixed in those colonial times, leaving him blind to the changing realities in China in the decades that followed. Luce was so taken with China's World War II leader, Chiang Kai-shek, that he wouldn't believe his own favorite reporter, Theodore White, when White wrote that Chiang's troops were corrupt and ineffective and were being soundly beaten by Mao Tse-tung's Communist army.

Luce despised communism and thought it was the United States' duty and destiny to defeat it. Even after Chiang's defeat and retreat to Taiwan, Luce's magazines hailed the Korean War as the start of World War III, proposing that Chiang be "unleashed" to help the United States defeat Russia and Mao once and for all. He nursed his obsessions with Chiang and communism all through the war in

Vietnam, skewing his magazines' coverage and undermining his once-formidable power in politics and public opinion.

Luce's mistake serves as a lesson to leaders of all stripes. If you make a concerted effort to keep up with cultural shifts—especially those in your own country, which may be even harder to see than changes that occur elsewhere—you can gain great tactical and strategic advantages.

Not long ago I won a small victory on the strength of my knowledge of Middle Eastern social customs. An owner's organization abruptly decided that it wanted to renegotiate his management contract with us. Our people were making slow progress in meetings with the owner, and we needed a faster way to get him to commit to a new contract.

When I was asked to join the negotiations, we organized a large and very public dinner to celebrate our longtime relationship with the owner. In effect, I imposed a deadline on the contract negotiations. If his issues remained unresolved when he appeared at the party, it would be a major embarrassment for him. Just hours before the dinner, the two teams sat down and hammered out an agreement, with concessions on both sides.

That night, in a starlit area of the hotel, 150 or so community members joined the owner, me, and the hotel staff for a spectacular meal full of Middle Eastern delicacies. The local newspapers carried photos of us together at the event, demonstrating to any doubters that our relationship was as strong as ever. The outcome, like the deal itself, was good for both sides, and the owner bore me no grudge for my pressure tactic.

In intercultural dealings, Americans often struggle to understand why negotiations run on well beyond what they consider reasonable. What they fail to comprehend is how the person across the table determines deadlines. By becoming familiar with the social customs of the party on the other side of the negotiating table, you may be able to put in place a deadline the same way I did.

While I was in Vietnam, I discovered that in some Asian cultures, the formal lines of authority often fail to reflect reality within any particular group. Later, when I took over as the general manager of the Copley Place Marriott in Boston, I came to realize that a seemingly skewed pecking order applied to our kitchen commissary crew, almost all of whom were Vietnamese.

It turned out that the person who actually ran the crew was not even on the organizational chart. So if I wanted something done, it would be a waste of breath to tell the executive in charge to make it happen. To get things done, I had to go to the informal leader. She was the one telling newcomers how things worked or demonstrating a better way to sear a steak or debone a fish. On the surface, she was just another crew member, but if you were appropriately respectful, she could orchestrate a great performance from all hands and settle any problems quickly.

To this day, I look for the informal structures and form relationships with their leaders. In my work with people from various cultures, it's the sure path to a more productive workforce.

Cultural understanding can improve your relationship with your employees, partners, and customers. To demonstrate that understanding, you might acknowledge a holiday not celebrated in the United States, for example, by making a remark in a meeting or in a note, or by having the company cafeteria serve a special meal. An approach I have employed and enjoyed throughout my career is to initiate a discussion of a country's history and customs. It works best if you have some knowledge already, because it shows your sincere interest and allows the other person to educate you about a favorite topic.

Cultural knowledge can also explain puzzling behaviors, including habits and attitudes you might find objectionable. An employee who hails from a country where littering is habitual may need more time to adjust to using recycling bins, and people from cultures where connections trump the legal system may tend to disregard your regulations. Foreign customers almost certainly will expect you to spend more personal time with them than you're accustomed to doing in the United States.

"BETTER" MAY BE IN THE EYE OF THE BEHOLDER

Two areas, in particular, tend to highlight the stark differences between the United States and certain other nations—the treatment of women and the workings of the legal system. Dealing with either demands extreme caution.

The status of women varies widely around the globe, ranging from haughty independence in France to near-chattel class in some Muslim cultures. When I first visited Japan in the 1970s, submissiveness was the rule. I would stand aside and wait for women to enter an elevator only to have them refuse until I went first. The Japanese have come a long way toward better treatment of women but they still have some distance to go, as I quickly became aware at a dinner in Tokyo a few years ago.

Nine of us sat around the table that night, eight Japanese bankers and me. The service was geisha style, conducted by a silent, efficient young woman. When the conversation lagged, I introduced the topic of Japanese history. I said I remembered two of the three ancient capitals, Kyoto and Edo, but couldn't recall the third.

"Hmmm" could be heard all around the table as they thought about my question. When no answer was forthcoming, the young woman spoke up. "It's Nara," she said. "Most Japanese men think we women don't know that," she added. Another "hmmm" could be heard as she left the room, followed by a deathly silence.

Realizing that I had caused trouble, I made it worse when I said, "I guess things are changing in Japan." One of my tablemates coldly replied, "Yes, and not always for the better."

The meal went on but with a different server, and I began to worry that I had cost the woman her job. I excused myself, ostensibly to go to the men's room. There she was outside the door guarding our shoes, clearly a punishment of sorts. I expressed my concern, but she assured me there was no problem. Her job was not in danger and, besides, as a second-year law student, she had other priorities. Yes, things are changing in Japan.

Caution flags should also be hoisted when it comes to foreign legal systems. They can make doing business overseas an exercise in frustration. Contracts that would automatically be enforced in the United States are ignored, and relationships rather than evidence often determine outcomes. Companies headquartered out of the country can face unexpected challenges.

Twenty years ago I was working closely with the owner of a hotel going up in New Delhi when a fire in a theater he owned killed hundreds of people. He knew he was liable for the disaster, and he disappeared. His family proceeded to sell the hotel to one of our competitors, a huge conglomerate called ITC, which promptly moved to force us out of the project.

"You can't do this," we protested. "We have a management contract."

Finally, I called Yogi Deveshwar, ITC's chairman and CEO, and a former classmate of mine in the advanced management program at the Harvard Business School. I thought we could settle the whole matter amicably, but Yogi knew better. "Ed," he said, "you're going to have to sue us."

Marriott had to look tough and strong, Yogi explained. Otherwise, Indian companies would take advantage of us, as had happened to another U.S.-based hotel chain. "We'll work this out in the long run," he said.

So we sued. Not only did the court rule that it could not decide the matter immediately, we were informed that it might take 20 years to get a decision. ITC, which won the right to operate the hotel until the case was resolved, gave us a management franchise for 10 years that enabled us to pay off our investment in the hotel.

We also received a substantial side benefit: Having proved our willingness to sue, we demonstrated that Marriott considered contractual agreements to be binding.

In some countries, we discovered 20 years ago that the police were not our friends. At one of our hotels, suspecting that there was a drug problem among our associates, we sent in a team of investigators to interview a number of people. The next morning, the local police entered the homes of every member of the hotel's executive committee as they were having breakfast and carted them off to jail. Only the general manager and the director of engineering escaped arrest because they were already at the hotel, and we quickly had them flown out of the country.

For three days, those who were arrested were transferred from one jail to another to evade our legal team. Finally the lawyers caught up with them and negotiated their release— on condition they would leave the country. Even though we presented evidence of drug dealing, none of the guilty employees were arrested.

That was how we learned that drug interests effectively controlled the local police and governor. We learned that if we discovered that an associate was involved with drugs, we should dismiss him for some other reason. And we learned to gain a thorough understanding of local law enforcement practices before we charged ahead, assuming that the American legal system was universally honored.

NUDGING CHANGE ALONG

Sometimes, it falls to a leader to nudge along cultural changes. When Vince Lombardi arrived in Green Bay, Wisconsin, early in 1959, the civil rights movement was in its infancy. Baseball had been integrated for years, as had most big-city football franchises, but Green Bay's population was mostly white and the Packers had signed very few black players. The few it did sign lived unhappily in Green Bay, enduring insults from the fans all too often.

Lombardi was determined to change the city's culture and tap football's expanding cadre of African-American talent. He signaled a new era by trading for Emlen Tunnell, an established defensive back from the New York Giants and a man no fan in his right mind would jeer. Lombardi also recruited Willie Wood, a star quarterback at the University of Southern California, to bolster the team's pass defense.

Early on, Wood made a mistake that his teammates ragged him about, telling him he would soon be on his way home. But when Lombardi heard the trash talk, he decisively put an end to it. "You're not going anywhere," he told the young man. "You're going to be here as long as I'm here."

Later, Wood credited Lombardi for giving him confidence. "I think it made a hell of a better ballplayer out of me," he said.

Inspired by Wood and Tunnell and the contributions they made toward changing the racial tone in Green Bay, I tried unsuccessfully to follow their lead at an Asian hotel we were managing. Given our fine working relationship with the owner, we believed we could strike a blow for equality by persuading him to accept a bright woman as his new general manager.

"Why are you doing this?" he demanded to know before adding: "Will she cry?"

We persevered, and eventually the woman got the job. She performed extremely well, but our relationship with the owner began to deteriorate. We couldn't figure out why until we discovered that the owner had often taken the previous manager to social events where the two men bonded. Bonding with the female general manager was not possible because the culture dictated that she sit beside the owner's wife at social events. Flexible pragmatism again won the day; we finally moved the woman to a new posting. There was nothing to be gained by pushing too hard, and, in any case, it wasn't our culture.

BRINGING IT HOME

Gaining an understanding of underlying historical cultural factors is obviously crucial to any leader engaged in international business. But it's no less important for managers who remain at home in our increasingly diverse country. Here's a rundown of the lessons I've learned over the years:

- *Do your homework.* In hiring and managing your team and dealing with customers and suppliers, take into account the background each person brings to the table.

Today, more and more of our domestic employees are drawn from other nations, and more and more of our operations take place overseas. Workplace diversity is not just a slogan but a reality.

Do enough research into history, customs, and cultures to have realistic expectations of the problems, conflicts, and opportunities these differences may present. Take time to talk to all of your people and enough of your customers to figure out where they're coming from, both literally and figuratively, and use these talks to learn more about each person's history and expectations.

- *Get the senior executives on board.* To make sure your top people appreciate the importance of cultural history and understanding, schedule your own domestic or overseas version of my Iron Bird Tours. There's no better way to introduce your people to the enormous variety of cultures involved in any business these days than first-hand exposure, however briefly, to any of them. They will get to see and hear how business is conducted in other countries, and how different priorities can be from what they may have expected.
- *Be realistic.* Learn to see what's really happening, both in the marketplace and in your own operation, and adjust to it. If your logo is green and your customers believe green is an unlucky color, change your logo. If there is an informal power structure in your workplace, figure out whether you can live with and profit by it before you attempt to stamp it out. And if you can benefit from an informal structure, tap it so long as you don't compromise your business or your ethics.
- *Use what you learn.* Turn cultural differences to your own advantage. When we learned that people in Asia favored

hotel settings for both business meals and family celebrations, we built hotels with more and larger restaurants than U.S. hotels typically offer. And when I had trouble negotiating with the owner of our hotel in the Middle East, I used my understanding of his culture to set up a *de facto* deadline for reaching a deal. If you are willing to make the effort, you can find similar cultural anomalies and customs that might give you an edge in dealing with various groups.

- *Always be flexible.* When operating abroad, adjust to the reality that the culture is not your culture and you're not responsible for it. You may be able to nudge along change when you think it's right, as we tried to do in putting a female general manager in charge in an Asian hotel. But if you fail as we did, you must face reality and accept it. It may go against your grain to honor cultural prejudices or work around an exasperating legal system, but as long as you're not violating your own basic values or breaking any U.S. laws, pragmatism is the first rule of business: Do what works.

Thus far, this book has focused on values, respect, trust, communicating with people, and leading by example—all in service to building strong relationships. In today's multicultural marketplace, as we have seen, dealing with cultural differences is a necessity for any business leader seeking to build and maintain the connections and relationships on which an enterprise depends. In Chapter 8, I discuss how you should go about maintaining those critical relationships.

Chapter 8 Cultivate Your Connections

Treasure your relationships, not your possessions.
                                        —Anonymous

A problem at one of our Thai hotels a few years ago required me to make several quick trips to visit the owner over a span of several months. As I should have expected, two other Bangkok owners heard about my visits and e-mailed to complain that I hadn't dropped by "to spend time with us." They were looking for what I call a relationship visit.

A leader devotes enormous time and energy to sowing and cultivating a garden of business relationships. The garden must be regularly watered and fed with the nutrients of respect and companionship to maintain and improve its quality. Neither you nor your company can afford to let the relationships you've planted go to seed—an all-too-common problem these days as technology strips the personal touch from our interactions. Whether the market is a difficult or a productive one, direct contact can have a huge impact on your associates and clients.

The disgruntled Thai owners were reminding me of the first rule of relationship maintenance—everyone needs face time. Notes and phone calls can buy you time, but they are only stopgap measures. To do the job right, you must get out from behind your desk and talk with your associates, partners, and customers—in person, face-to-face. Nothing less will do.

You'll find that the payback is well worth the trouble. Solid relationships are the cornerstone of success, in business as in life. In the later years of his phenomenal coaching career, Bear Bryant showed that he cared deeply about his players as individuals, not just as the star quarterback or punter or wide receiver on one of his famously winning football teams. Bryant advised the young men to mind their manners, respect their parents, and plan for the future—and he promised to help them realize their dreams.

In the rebellious 1970s, Bryant even learned to live with players who used hair dryers in the locker room to style their collar-length locks. They, in turn, learned to live with his acute sense of discipline. The relationships Bryant forged with his players were strong enough to withstand considerable stress—and extraordinary talent didn't exempt a player from following Bear's rules.

Bryant called Joe Namath "the greatest athlete I ever coached," and others thought so, too. Namath would win fame as the New York Jets quarterback who led his team to one of the greatest upsets in sports history. The Jets put the "super" in Super Bowl III when they beat the heavily favored Baltimore Colts, 16 to 7.

But Namath got no breaks from Bryant. When he violated training rules, the coach benched him for two games, one of which was the Sugar Bowl. Namath could have quit the team and accepted an offer to play in Canada, but he stayed at Alabama. "Coach Bryant was right," he said later. "When he spanked you, you knew it was because he loved you."

Leaders and their teams alike yearn for that kind of strong, trusting relationship.

Reassurance was what our two Bangkok owners were looking for when they raised their complaint. Their confidence somewhat shaken because Marriott was opening new hotels in their city, they needed to hear that their properties would not be pushed to the sidelines. Our Asia executives made special trips to see them, but the owners wouldn't feel completely relieved until I spoke to them directly.

On my next trip to Bangkok, I arranged to have a dinner and a lunch with each of the owners separately. As is our custom, the conversation during the meal was relaxed, friendly, and devoid of business issues. Later, when we got around to business, I let them know that I understood their anxiety. But I also reminded them that we manage multiple properties in major cities all around the world. For instance, in the Atlanta area alone, we operate nearly 100 hotels displaying various Marriott brands, and we do it with minimal overlap. Finally, I pledged to continue marshaling our superior resources in support of their particular properties.

Since that minor rift, our well-tended relationship garden has continued to produce a cornucopia of mutual benefits, a particularly welcome asset during recent moments of political unrest in Thailand.

HOW TO TEND YOUR GARDEN

To cultivate your relationships, you need to reorganize your schedule to make time for personal contacts. It takes a conscious effort to overcome the pressure of everyday problems and deadlines. In my case, I put together elaborate itineraries that expose me to the maximum number of people in the minimum amount of time. Here's a typical schedule from a recent 10-day tour:

- Los Angeles to London for special event, introducing Prince's Rainforest Project hosted by the Prince of Wales, along with visits to three of our hotels.
- London to Singapore for dinner meeting with owner nervous about regional personnel changes. Gave speech to meeting of international Visa executives (some of our best customers).
- Singapore to Hong Kong for discussions (over dinner) with developer upset about recent events in China.

- Hong Kong to Jakarta for third visit to owners and staff since July 2009 terrorist bombing (formal meeting plus lunch).
- Jakarta to Dubai to drop off luggage en route to dinner in Doha, Qatar, with owners of our three newest hotels there.
- Doha back to Dubai to reunite with luggage, attend ceremony marking opening of new regional office, visit with potential new partner, and dinner with owner of 20 years.

In the course of that trip, I played several different roles. In London, I represented the company at an event benefiting the environment, largely a public relations function. I also met with our local executives and general managers and touched base with the hotels' associates, thus fulfilling my operational responsibilities.

In Singapore and Hong Kong, I wore my troubleshooter hat, helping to sort out the owners' problems. In Jakarta, I showed our continuing concern in the aftermath of the bombing. In Dubai I was a salesman, meeting with an owner who was considering putting several of his hotels under a single brand rather than running each one independently.

Relationship building is a skill that can be learned and mastered, but some people perfect their technique more easily than others. Kathleen Matthews, Marriott International's executive vice president for global communications and public affairs, is one such person. Kathleen, who came to Marriott after spending three decades as a reporter and television anchor, develops business and personal relationships through her social circle, which she nurtures assiduously. Judicious in asking for favors but generous in dispensing them, she has built a network that includes Nancy Reagan and Hillary Clinton along with a cadre of ambassadors that stretch from China to Colombia. Kathleen's ever-expanding network is enormously useful to Marriott as she nudges high-ranking figures to give us entry into high-level government circles.

Even in the United States, where relationships tend to congeal fairly rapidly, it takes time and effort to reach a solid level of trust. The challenge is much more complex overseas. Witness our experience in Jordan.

I first visited the kingdom in 1978, when we were building a hotel in the capital city of Amman. The general manager was an exceptionally affable former race-car driver named Haile Aguilar. Haile, who could get along with just about anyone, turned the hotel into a major social center. Among his regular customers was Prince Abdullah, the son of King Hussein.

Haile and Abdullah participated in the Rally races together and became very close friends. Over the years, Marriott was able to build on Haile's connection with the royal family, and King Hussein and Queen Noor would celebrate special events at the Amman Marriott.

The Muasher family, who are the major shareholders in the owning companies of Jordan's three Marriott hotels, is a renowned family known for its loyalty and closeness to the royal family. Over the years several of its members have served in the Jordanian government. Dr. Rajai Musaher, the present elder of the family served as a minister of economy several times and today is the Deputy Prime Minister. Whereas Dr. Marwan Muasher opened the first Jordanian Embassy in Israel in 1996; he served as an Ambassador to the United States and participated in negotiating the pretrade agreement between the United States and Jordan. He has been a Foreign Minister and a Deputy Prime Minister. Nadim Muasher oversees hotels and other businesses in Jordan, and has responsibility for the three

Marriotts, a Sheraton in Amman, and is building the new JW Marriott in Aqaba. I have worked with Nadim for over 20 years and hold him in the highest regard. We prize our relationship with the family, recognizing it as one of the closest connections we've formed in the 40 years I've been involved with Marriott.

I truly admired King Hussein, who died in 1999. He remained a loyal friend to the United States even amid growing turbulent dislike toward America from the millions of Palestinian and other Arab immigrants residing in Jordan. Abdullah, who succeeded his father as king, strives to maintain the same balancing act. He, too, has proved to be a strong leader in an incredibly challenging political environment.

Our relationship with Jordan's royal family and the Muasher family has continued to strengthen in recent years, and we have made efforts large and small to make it happen. A few years back, I found myself in conversation with King Abdullah and U.S. Secretary of State Colin Powell, who was in town for a global economic forum at the Jordan Valley Marriott. As we stood in the lobby chatting amiably, the king mentioned that, in his experience, our hotel had the best spa in the Middle East. He urged Secretary Powell to try it. Powell explained that he had been unable to book rooms for his delegation at the Marriott because none were available. Seeing an opening to prove King Abdullah's point while also pleasing Powell, I wasted no time in inviting the secretary to use the spa whenever he wished. Who am I to let a room shortage get in the way of international diplomacy?

Despite our diligent efforts to maintain and deepen the relationship among Marriott, the Muasher family, and the king, we still can't compete with Haile Aguilar. If you were to ask Abdullah to comment on Marriott, he would acknowledge the long-standing relationship, and, with prompting, he might remember the five times he and I have met. But mention Haile and he'll beam as he recounts their friendship.

The lesson: You can build strong business relationships, but they will never rise to the level of long-term personal friendships. We value our relationship with Haile Aguilar in any case. He's a good man to know for many reasons.

TOUCHING BASE

In a world that daily becomes less personal as technology expands its grip on the medium of human exchange, forming productive relationships with business associates can give you a competitive advantage. Outside of the United States and a few other Western countries, relationships are the single most important badge of entry into the realm of successful businessmen and -women. Become adept at relationship building and you will have an easier time solving problems, building your business, and increasing your profits.

U.S. companies operating in China today confront the most difficult kind of business environment—constant flux. Signed and sealed contracts may be suddenly repudiated as a new partner jumps ship for a richer offer. Local and/or national regulations may be in full force one day and ignored the next. As Marriott has discovered, it is next to impossible to predict even the near term, much less plan confidently for the long-range future.

In a recent *Wall Street Journal* essay, Denis F. Simon and Leonard M. Fuld point out that the best way to keep abreast of upcoming changes in Chinese business is to nurture good *Guanzi*—good relationships—with those in the know.

Dr. Simon is a professor of international affairs at Penn State University, and Fuld is the founder of a Massachusetts research and consulting firm. "We believe," they write, "it is critically important for western managers to continually build and cultivate extensive networks of government and industry contacts who have the power to help corporate projects and ventures succeed."

Part of the difficulty of doing business in China is the disconnect between the central government and the various governmental units in different parts of the country. It's not enough to build relationships with a few top officials in Beijing, the authors point out. Westerners need to stay in touch with local officials as well, and to maintain connections with local suppliers and salespeople who can provide "firsthand knowledge" of forthcoming developments in their areas.

One radical change has added to the problems facing Western companies trying to set up shop in China. In spite of the huge increase in the number of college-educated Chinese, the country's businesses have encountered a shortage of top-level talent. As a result, government agencies and provincial governments have dispatched delegations to the United States and Europe seeking to convince Chinese technical experts to return home. They are now offering wages equal to those the Western companies provide, an abrupt departure from the past.

The net result is to pit Chinese and Western businesses against each other in a struggle to hire the best people. That can be a major hassle, especially if you're trying to establish a research and development organization. Once again, you can get a leg up on the problem by cultivating your connections with the local people you do business with. They can point your way toward potential new hires including those who are unhappy with their current employers.

In the Western world, too, the right relationships can give you a distinct advantage with customers, suppliers, and employees.

Costco founder and CEO Jim Sinegal makes a point of staying in touch with his employees. He ditches his desk and hops on his corporate jet to go visiting, stopping in at about a dozen Costco outlets a day. With 570 warehouses scattered across the United States, Mexico, Puerto Rico, Canada, the United Kingdom, Taiwan, Korea, Japan, and Australia, Sinegal is never at a loss for people and places to visit.

And he loves it, likening his job to show business. Little wonder given that the Costco employees he visits treat him like a rock star. They like the boss, and he returns the affection. His multicultural employees "know that I want to say hello to them, because I like them," he says. Sounding a more serious tone in an ABC News profile a few years back, Sinegal opined that "no manager and no staff in any business feels very good if the boss is not interested enough to come and see them." My philosophy exactly.

Sinegal, whose Issaquah, Washington-based company counts 57.2 million cardholders and fiscal 2009 revenue of $71.4 billion (the year ended in August of 2009), is not your typical business titan. Casual, friendly, and unassuming, you might mistake him for a clerk if you bumped into him in the meat department or the electronics section at one of Costco's warehouse stores. The name tag he wears doesn't say "Jim, the Costco CEO" or "Jim, the company founder," or even "Jim Sinegal." He simply identifies himself as "Jim." The son of a steelworker, Sinegal's working-class values inform the corporate culture, and right from the start in 1983, the boss insisted that everyone would be on a first-name basis, just like a family.

Costco's employee turnover and theft rates are extremely low, but it's not just the backslapping and chit-chat that keeps Jim Sinegal's workers loyal and happy. He pays his people extremely well and gives them better-than-average benefits, including health coverage. Wall Street perennially complains about Sinegal's benevolence, but he dismisses the analysts' Scrooge-like advice as shortsighted. "Our code of ethics says we have to obey the law," Sinegal declares. "We have to take care of our customers, take care of our people. And if we do those things, we think that we'll reward our shareholders."

Time has proved the validity of Sinegal's credo. From its July 10, 1986, closing price of $10.19 a share, adjusted for stock splits and dividends, to its prerecession peak of $73.27 a share on May 12, 2008, Costco's stock price had climbed by more than 600 percent. The stock touched its recessionary low price of $38.98 on March 9, 2009, and has since climbed back into the mid-$50s.

Sinegal points out that Costco, which is the largest membership warehouse club and the third-largest retailer overall in the United States, not to mention the biggest retailer of fine wines, doesn't have a public relations department and spends little on advertising. What the company does have are 149,500 loyal employees plus 57-million-plus satisfied cardholders who double as goodwill ambassadors, bragging to their friends and neighbors about the advantages of being a Costco employee or customer.

In his everyman sort of way, Jim Sinegal might say that you can't beat that with a stick.

There is one program any company can employ that has the potential to create and nurture strong relationships with every stakeholder, including both employees and customers. These days it generally travels under the rubric of "social responsibility," and there are those in the business community who think it's a waste of shareholders' money—money they think might better be spent on dividends. I beg to differ. Properly handled, programs to support local communities or improve your company's "green" impact, for instance, can yield major advantages, both tangible and intangible.

I have seen those advantages firsthand. That's because Marriott has made social responsibility part of its core mission. It has pledged that "every community will be a better place to live and work because we are there." And we have backed that pledge by transforming dozens of processes and procedures within our individual hotels and supporting dozens of programs and projects to help the less fortunate and improve the environment all over the world.

I have seen how this work has strengthened Marriott's relationship with employees and associates, increasing their pride in the company—and thus their feelings of self-worth. I have seen how it improves our connections with owners and franchisees, demonstrating our commitment to their communities. I have seen how it impresses the guests of our hotels, sustaining and enlarging the company's reputation as a responsible, civic-minded organization.

To make certain that our dedication to social responsibility doesn't flag, it has been built into our corporate structure. It is an automatic part of the agenda at meetings of the business councils, the gatherings of hotel general managers in various parts of the world. The GMs are then responsible for implementing social initiatives at their properties. Those hotels that excel in that work receive a variety of awards and honors at division and company-wide meetings. Executives' success in promoting social responsibility efforts is rewarded in their paychecks.

Because Marriott is in the business of providing guests with housing and food, the company has focused its community efforts on providing housing and food for those in need. Over the past 13 years, for example, we and our employees and customers, in partnership with Habitat for Humanity International, have helped finance and build thousands of homes in 15 countries. I have personally taken part in Habitat projects in Costa Rica, Honolulu, and Thailand—and used Habitat sites as part of a team-building program with my executive committee. The Fairfield Inn brand has made Habitat for Humanity its signature community service activity; house builds are an integral part of its major events, including general manager, owner, and franchisee conferences.

Marriott has long contributed both food and cash to hunger relief organizations in dozens of countries. In the United States, it partners with Feeding America, the former Second Harvest. We also encourage our managers and employees to volunteer at food banks.

The Marriott family has been a major supporter of programs to aid children who confront physical and/or economic hardship. The family foundation created "Bridges . . . from School to Work" in 1989 to provide training and secure jobs for special education school graduates. More than 11,500 of these youngsters with disabilities have gone through the program, finding work with 3,400 employers, including Marriott. The company is also a leader in the Youth Career Initiative, a project of Prince Charles's International Tourism Partnership (ITP). (I have been chairman of ITP for nine years.) High school graduates with little or no chance of finding jobs go through an intensive, six-month program at participating hotel chains, learning skills to prepare them for jobs that would otherwise have been beyond them. And the company is a key underwriter of Safe Kids Worldwide, which seeks to prevent the unintentional injury of children 14 and under. In China, for example, it emphasizes fire prevention because fires are a leading cause of death and disability for children of those ages.

A standing committee of the board of directors is dedicated to achieving maximum diversity throughout Marriott's operations. One of its initiatives has increased the number of company hotels owned by minorities or women by more than 25 percent in the past five years. Similar programs have been undertaken with suppliers, customers, and employees. For example, the company has tripled the amount spent with minority, women, and LGBT suppliers since 2005.

Marriott's green initiative has been felt in every corner of the company. In the hotels, plastic key cards and pens, produced by Bic to be biodegradable in five years, as well as traditional towels and toilet paper have yielded to more environmentally friendly products. Energy consumption has been reduced by installing low-flow shower heads and changing extended-stay guests' linens every third day rather than daily. Instead of automatically delivering newspapers to each guestroom, Marriott now asks guests to request a paper or pick one up in the lobby. The estimated annual savings in the quantity of waste to be recycled, company-wide: 18 million papers.

A global green council made up of senior executives, which I have cochaired with Arne Sorenson and Kathleen Matthews, has established a set of goals that include reducing energy and water consumption by 25 percent per available room by 2017. The company works with owners and franchisers to encourage the purchase of energy-efficient equipment and with suppliers to improve the energy efficiency of their operations. We urge the sponsors of meetings and conferences at our hotels to adopt green practices—everything from recycle bins in the rooms to organic flowers and reusable name tags—and they have responded enthusiastically.

The company also contributes financially to environmental organizations. For example, we have entered into an unprecedented partnership with a Brazilian state and a private foundation to protect 1.4 million acres of Amazonian rain forest. And 5 percent of the total cost of guest rooms booked for a group meeting at many of our hotels is earmarked for preserving the rain forest.

The many ways by which the company seeks to meet its social responsibility—indeed, the social responsibility mission itself—are not based on the personal likes or dislikes of our leaders. Marriott is a profit-making organization, and its actions are intended to serve its commercial purposes—and so they do. They cement existing relationships and encourage new ones that benefit the bottom line.

The same is true of any business relationship. Staying in touch with associates and customers is a corporate necessity, not a matter of personal choice. Obviously, if you enjoy spending time with your business acquaintances, that's all for the good. But it's not a requirement.

Publisher Henry Luce always relished his relationships with the reporters, writers, and editors of his *Time*, *Life*, and *Fortune* magazines. He grilled his people relentlessly for new facts and ideas, engaging them in lively debates over the issues of the day. But he strained those relationships by using the magazines as propaganda machines to boost his heroes, including Chinese leader Chiang Kai-shek and U.S. Army General Douglas MacArthur, and to promote political causes, including the war in Vietnam and the Republican Party.

Time's shameless bias in favor of Dwight D. Eisenhower in the presidential election of 1952 pushed Luce's editors to the brink. When the boss took them to dinner, they were expecting an apology and reconciliation. Instead, he gave a rambling, off-the-cuff harangue that completely soured his relationship with most of his editors. "Though it has never been said to you before, I'm your boss," he announced. "I guess that means I can fire any of you. . . . But I don't know anybody who can fire me. Sometimes I wish there were." From that day forward, most of his people kept Luce at arm's length.

Was the speech necessary? Maybe. Luce had no intention of changing his behavior and honesty is the first rule of any relationship, so there was little else he could say. But the tone of his speech, and the behavior that incited the crisis in the first place, were off base. Luce knew, or certainly should have known, that the talented reporters and editors he depended on highly valued their objectivity. His biases undermined those values.

In my case—and I hope in yours, as well—I discovered early on that my associates and I shared the same objectives, making it both enjoyable and profitable to stay in touch. I relish the give-and-take and the chance to catch up with people at home and abroad. I also learn things—new approaches to tasks that can be shared with other parts of the organization, new problems that call for resolution. Had I not taken time out to maintain my connections, I would have missed so much that is new, important, and pleasurable.

Associates, customers, and partners all like to be recognized for contributing to your shared enterprise. When a leader comes out of the executive suite and steps into the workplace to reconnect with people, it can be an extremely powerful form of acknowledgment. When you spend a few days visiting branch offices, talking with customers, or taking partners out to dinner, you can immeasurably strengthen the ties that bind these people to your company.

First, though, comes the relationship itself. In this book, I have suggested ways in which you can establish your relationships and set the ground rules for achieving a productive business connection, regardless of the country or culture of the people with whom you work. You will want to start with a value system that will support your efforts and delineate the ethical boundaries within which your relationships can develop. That value system will foster mutual respect, thereby promoting the trust and loyalty that will allow you to communicate effectively, lead by example, and transcend cultural and historic differences.

Of course, some leaders, even certifiable geniuses, have personal qualities that make relationships hard to forge and maintain. Walt Disney, you will recall, was a micromanaging and disparaging boss who antagonized his associates, thus triggering resentment that boiled over in his studio. Disney's self-delusion compounded his problems. He saw himself as a benevolent patriarch and couldn't understand why his people were unhappy. A leader who sees his or her flaws more clearly can find ways to offset them.

Consider Steve Jobs. The visionary CEO of Apple is famous for his showmanship, his eye for talent, and his genuine charisma. Yet he has also been described as an indifferent manager, willful, secretive, overly conscious of his own brainpower, and capable of firing people in sudden tantrums—qualities that make for uneasy, difficult connections with others.

Jobs, however, has compensated by finding an anti-Jobs as his number two man. Tim Cook, Apple's chief operating officer, is unemotional, contained, quiet, and private—though just as devoted as the boss himself. Recruited from Compaq in 1998, Cook rapidly cleaned up Apple's supply, manufacturing, and distribution chain, cut costly inventory, and began posting gross profit margins that have lately topped 35 percent. Cool, but also firm with his people, Cook has run the company smoothly for six months at a stretch during Jobs' recent illnesses.

Although some Apple employees and associates are still terrified to ride in an elevator with Jobs, his problematic qualities are no longer on the loose in ways that harm the company—and his people can still idolize him at a distance. Some joke that if Cook ever became CEO, he'd have to find an anti-Cook to play Jobs' role.

More than most, Captain Mike Abrashoff found the magic formula for establishing a strong, productive relationship with his team aboard *Benfold*. Although he was a master at communicating with his sailors, at soliciting their input and listening hard, what really gained their respect and trust was his willingness to show them by example the kind of behavior he was looking for.

He understood that if you want your team to change their ways, you can't do it with e-mail and speeches alone. You have to be personally involved in moving the tape.

Abrashoff, as we saw in Chapter 5, taught his officers to stop pulling rank by joining the sailors on the lower deck. But his willingness to put himself on the line, as it were, extended to virtually every aspect of life on the ship.

When a sailor suggested the use of stainless-steel nuts, bolts, and rivets as a way of cutting back on the crew's endless task of chipping and painting the ship, Abrashoff decided to give it a try. When his aides were unable to find the items in the Navy supply system, the captain went shopping at stores such as Home Depot with the ship's credit card in hand. He spent thousands of dollars on the fasteners, and once they were installed, they put off chipping and painting for almost a full year. Today, the whole navy uses stainless-steel fasteners.

That kind of hands-on behavior sent a message of hope and achievement to the crew. It made them understand that the captain was on their side, working to improve their working conditions and the ship's performance. And that helped inspire them to come up with important, innovative ideas. Some of them actually led Abrashoff to move beyond some of the items in the Navy's training manual, which in turn brought *Benfold* a remarkable success: a retraining process that the Navy claimed would take six months was completed in just one week.

BRINGING IT HOME

Business relationships sometimes bear little resemblance to personal relationships. You may have absolutely nothing else in common with a business partner or associate other than the business. And when that's the case, it can be difficult to spend time relaxing and making small talk as I did with some of our owners.

If you obviously don't have any shared interests, don't make the conversation unbearably awkward by pretending otherwise. But if you can find some common ground—hobbies, children and family, books, travel—spending a little time talking about noncontroversial subjects can break the ice and make it easier to talk about problem areas or an associate's dissatisfaction when the time comes.

Beyond that potential stumbling block, here are some lessons I've learned about building relationships:

- *Tend to your garden.* It's a waste of time and effort to forge relationships with associates if you don't have any intention of nurturing them from time to time. Just like personal friendships, business associates need to know you haven't lost interest in their challenges and successes. Sometimes they need your advice, at other times they need you to acknowledge their achievements—and on occasion, they simply need to know that you haven't forgotten them altogether.

Our Bangkok owners got a little nervous thinking they might be overshadowed by our new venture. Who could blame them? When people acquire a new car or even a new pair of shoes, they typically show off the new purchase, leaving the old car in the garage and the old shoes in the closet. From time to time, your associates will need a relationship visit. An e-mail or a phone call can buy you some time, but it won't stave off deep-seated anxieties. Only you, in person, can shore up your business relationships.

In developing countries like China, where the business environment is in constant flux and rules and regulations can change overnight, relationships with local people are especially vital. They are likely to know better than any outsider when a change is in the wind and how best to prepare for it.

- *Schedule it.* No matter how sincere you are when you promise to visit your associates in their places of business, it's doubtful that you will fulfill those commitments unless you put them on your schedule and stick to it. Everyday problems have a way of pushing us off our intended course. "How can I leave now?" you think when crisis flares. But let's face it, not one moment of your day is truly foreseeable; the unexpected occurs with regularity. The solution is to schedule personal contacts and give them the same degree of importance as your other business dealings.

I make the best use of my time by making schedules that allow me to touch base with multiple associates on any given trip. Hopscotching from one situation to another might seem disorienting at first, but with practice, it gets easier.

• *Enjoy the benefits.* You don't have to personally like your business associates, but you do have to maintain regular contact with them if you hope to prosper. Strong business relationships can give you a competitive advantage, and face-to-face contact is especially valued in an era when impersonal technological communications dominate. Problem solving is infinitely more complex.

I recently witnessed a bit of social negotiation between two people in their early thirties that proves my point. The text messaging went back and forth for the better part of a day. Are we meeting for dinner? Where will we meet? What time should we arrive? Should I make reservations or will you? Each exchange seemed to surface new issues. All I could think was, "Why don't you just pick up the phone and talk to each other until all the details are ironed out?" A whole day of dithering could have been eliminated by two minutes of actual conversation. Such is the exasperation built into much of today's technology. Counteract the drawbacks by setting aside more time for personal contact.

• *Keep your eyes wide open.* Seeing ourselves clearly is no easy task. But flaws unnoticed can sour business relationships and send your valuable human assets fleeing. Walt Disney was notoriously blind to his faults, and it cost him dearly. His studio was plagued with labor problems, and his reputation for genius was tarnished by his poor treatment of talented artists.

Another genius, Steve Jobs, is reputed to be equally diffi-cult at times, but with a difference: Jobs had the good sense to put COO Tim Cook between him and his business part-ners and associates. The cool and contained Cook stepped in to repair Apple's broken relationships with suppliers, manu-facturers, and distributors. Expanding profits followed.

You've read pretty much all I have to say about nearly 40 years spent building an international business. Given the scope of our properties, my stories are probably more exotic than what you'll read from most businesspeople. But whether you're based in Chicago or Calcutta, Ithaca or Istanbul, I hope the lessons I've learned and shared will expand your business acumen and increase the pleasure and profits you derive from whatever it is you do.

Thank you for sticking with me, and *Adios, Auf Wieder-sehen, Au revoir, Lar-korn, Sayonara, Selamat-tingaal*—and that's just the beginning!

Afterword

Previous pages aside, leadership is not something you accomplish by reading a book or sitting in your office. It's something you learn and hone by doing—though I hope that the experiences I've shared here, and the lessons I've learned from those experiences, will set you on a more productive course.

Learning is or should be a lifelong endeavor. I was fortunate to begin my education in the art of leadership and relationship building under the tutelage of memorable teachers like Sergeant James at the Prudential Center in Boston and my Sigma Alpha Epsilon fraternity brothers at Boston University. Then, when I began my active military duty, I learned from the best teachers the U.S. Army had to offer. In the inimitable military style, they made sure we remembered what we were taught—because a lapse of memory on the battlefield was all too often a soldier's last.

I have come to see trust as a major ingredient of a personal relationship. Take my friend Buck Laird. Buck and I have been friends for almost 40 years. On two occasions Buck has called and asked, "Do you trust me?" What Buck had in mind were investments that I saw for the first time when I flew to Hawaii to sign the contracts. The initial 30-acre deal occurred in the 1970s. At some point, you need to rely on trust to cement your relationships. Such connections can be profitable—and my ventures were.

Partly because of my military background, Marriott decided to take a chance on me. I was hired as a management trainee in 1972 and spent the next 39 years learning— everything from cleaning potatoes to cleaning rooms and lessons in marketing, sales, and operations. As a result, I came to see how the work our associates performed at every level is so crucial, and how important it is to build and nurture connections across the board.

Since that time I have visited more than 150 countries on six continents and launched the careers of 72,000 associates. But the most important and rewarding piece has been the chance to meet a multicultural band of wonderful people with whom I have developed lasting relationships. Customers, owners, partners, associates, and government officials have all contributed their unique perspective and slice of color to a multicultural portrait of adventure, excitement, and friendship.

Today, Marriott International has more than 500 hotels open or under construction outside the United States and 400-plus individual owners. When I started, we had only 16 properties abroad. I no longer have full responsibility for our global partnerships and associations. Other talented executives have taken on the key roles as relationship officers for our hotels—although I still remain involved in many of the connections we've made and nurtured over more than two decades. Old habits die hard.

As I come to the end of this particular part of my story, I can't let you close the book without paying tribute to some of the people and mentors who have made my career possible. Bill Shaw, Al LeFaivre, Paul Reed, and Bill Tiefel have taught me a great deal and stood by me through almost

40 years of good times and bad. My peers and associates have helped and supported me in my pioneering journey to expand
Marriott's presence to the far corners of the globe.

More than anyone else, though, my guiding light has been Bill Marriott Jr., a man who embodies true leadership. Rarely does the son of a great leader become a great leader himself. The Marriotts, father and son, are the exception.

Bill Jr. has made it possible for me to gain a unique understanding of business practices around the world, providing the platform, values, and mechanisms that allowed me to model the behaviors I have recommended in the previous pages. In fact, you might say that whatever helpful advice you found there is owing to Bill's leadership. I quote his favorite saying frequently to my direct reports: "Success is never final."

And so, after 10 million miles' worth of experiences, insights, stories, and just plain fun, my odyssey with Marriott is drawing to close. I look forward with enthusiasm to the next adventure.

About the Author

Edwin D. "Ed" Fuller is president and managing director of international lodging for Marriott International Inc. Based at the company's headquarters in Washington, DC, he has been in charge of international lodging since 1990. Under his leadership, the business has grown from 16 properties outside the United States and Canada to 400 hotels in 70 countries with another 175 hotels under construction.

Mr. Fuller joined Marriott in 1972 as a management trainee and has held numerous positions of increasing marketing, sales, and operational responsibility. These include the director of national and international sales and reservations; chief sales and marketing officer for Marriott International, and opening general manager of the Long Island (New York) Marriott and the Boston Marriott Copley Place hotels. In 1985, he was named regional vice president for Marriott's Midwest Region, based in Chicago; four years later, he was appointed regional vice president for the Western/Pacific Region, based in Santa Ana, California. He assumed leadership of Marriott's international lodging operations in 1990 as senior vice president and managing director and was later promoted to executive vice president and managing director. He was promoted to president and managing director, his current position, in 1997. He has been a corporate officer since 1990 and an executive corporate officer since 1997.

Earlier in his career, Mr. Fuller was credited with establishing Marriott International's original international reservations network and for its global sales and marketing organization. He served as a board member and chairman of SNR International, a reservations consortium based in Zurich.

Mr. Fuller attended Wake Forest University and is a 1968 graduate of Boston University. He is a graduate of the Harvard Graduate School of Business advanced management program. He served in the U.S. Army as a captain in Germany and Vietnam and was awarded the Bronze Star and the Army Commendation Medal.

An active alumnus of Boston University, Mr. Fuller is a former president of its alumni association and a former trustee of the university. He currently serves on the advisory boards of its School of Hospitality and Business. He is chairman of the School of Hospitality Advisory Board. He also serves on the university's International Advisory Board. In 1998, he received the Alumni Award, the university's highest recognition. He recently was appointed to the Board of Overseers of Boston University. He also serves as chairman of the Advisory Board for the University of California Irvine, the Paul Merage School of Business. He is a trustee of the University of California Irvine Foundation. He was recently appointed to the California State University System's Hospitality Industry Advisory Board. He is a trustee of the International Business Leaders Forum, founded by the Prince of Wales; chairs the Governing Council of the International Tourism Partnership; and currently serves on the Safe Kids Worldwide Board of Directors and the Pacific Area Travel Association Foundation

Board of Directors, as well as the Editorial Advisory Boards of *TravelAge West* and GlobalHotelNetwork.com. Earlier this year, he was named a commissioner of travel and tourism for the State of California. He is a past member of the Corporate Advisory Board of Safe Kids Worldwide and a former director of the United Way International Board. In 2008, he received the China Hotel Investment Summit 2008 Lifetime Achievement Award, and the Aatithya Ratna Award at the Hotel Investment Forum India in 2011.

Index